ES'S SQUARE

't North sides in 1821

rt North sides in 1930

ct North sides in 1986

ST JAMES'S SQUARE

People · Houses · Happenings

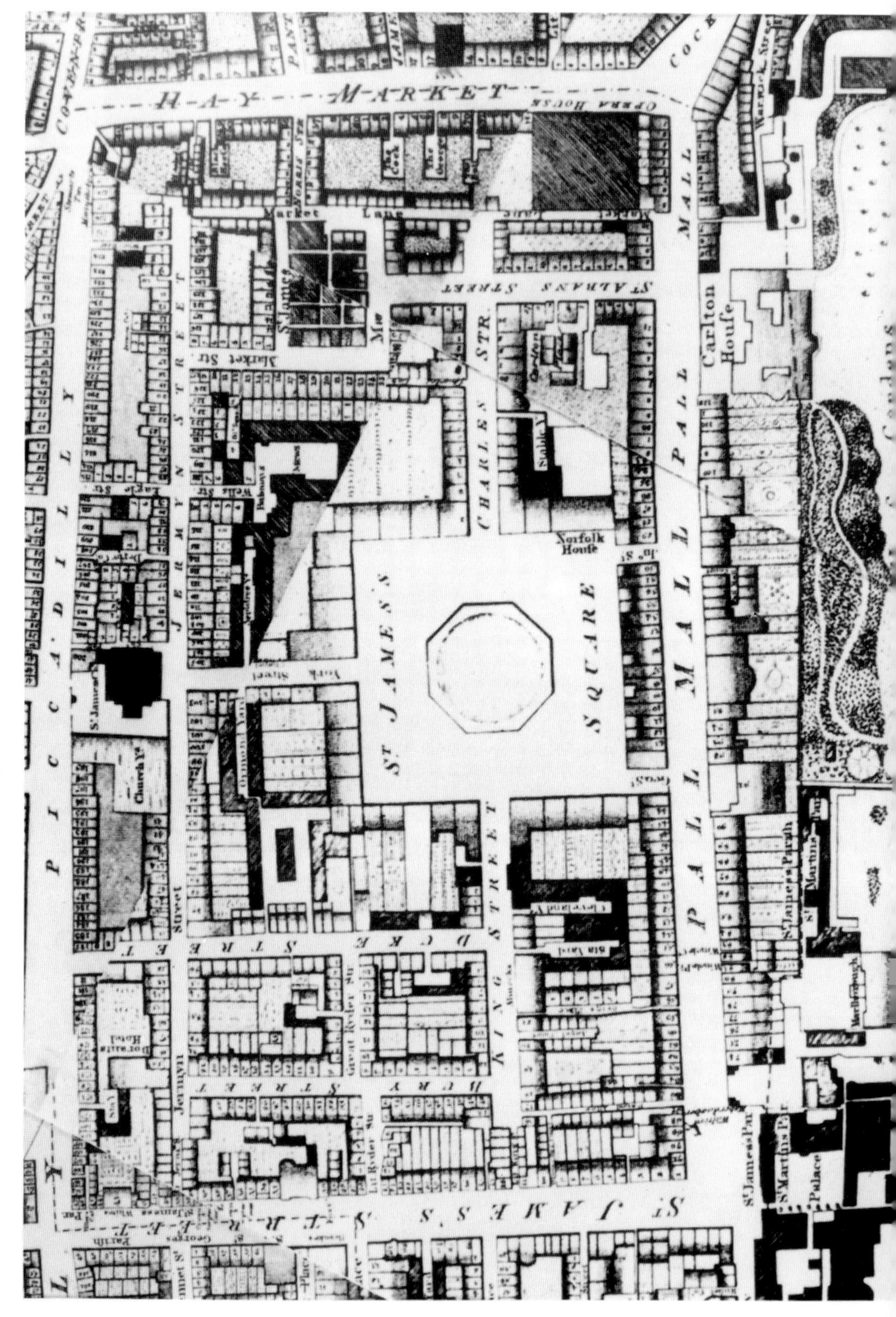

St James's Square and neighbourhood. Horwood's Map of 1792–99.

ST JAMES'S SQUARE

People · Houses · Happenings

Denys Forrest

She shall have all that's fine and fair
   And the best of silk and sattin shall wear;
And ride in a coach and take the air
   And have a house in St James's Square.

— *The Duke of Leeds' footman (1740)*

QUILLER PRESS
London

The following St James's Square firms and organizations have contributed towards the cost of the production of this book:

National Westminster Bank plc
D'Arcy Masius Benton & Bowles
James Buchanan & Co. Ltd
RTZ Services Ltd
Associated Oiltools Inc.
Richard Ellis
Grindlays Bank Ltd
Clerical, Medical & General Life Assurance Society
East India, Devonshire, Sports and Public Schools Club
Hawker Siddeley Group Ltd
Prudential Assurance Co.
Winchester House Property Co. Ltd
Army & Navy Club
Chem Systems International Ltd
Lamco Paper Sales Ltd
Goddard Kay Rogers & Associates Ltd
Consolidated Gold Fields plc
Charterhall plc

In addition a generous contribution was received from de Morgan & Co.

Published by Quiller Press Limited
46 Lillie Road
London
SW6 1TN

First published 1986
This edition published 2001

ISBN 1 899163 72 7

Printed through Colorcraft, Hong Kong

Contents

List of Illustrations

Colour plates

Between pages 102 and 103

Acknowledgements

As readers of this book will quickly perceive, its appearance has been much enhanced by the delightful chapter head drawings of Theodore Ramos. The garden plans (pp. 87 and 154) were drawn by Gill Roker, who also played a valuable part in marshalling the illustrations.

On the side of research, the Archives and Local History section of Westminster Public Libraries (archivist, Miss M. J. Swarbrick) is mentioned opposite by Mr Hill, but it was hardly less valuable to the author to be made free of the London Library, so appropriately sited at No. 14 St James's Square and with a Trustee (Mr Douglas Matthews) as Librarian.

Other libraries and institutions which were generous with help include the British, Guildhall, RIBA, Huntington (California) and Brighton Reference Libraries, the Courtauld Institute, National Portrait Gallery, Imperial War Museum and the Survey of London (Mr John Bezodis).

As regards individual houses in the Square there can be only a general, though heartfelt, acknowledgement of the unfailing support given to the project by past and present owners and tenants, headed of course by the whole body of the current Trustees, as named in Appendix 1. But among older connections with the Square, special mention should perhaps be made of Lord Boyd of Merton, the last 'Guinness' Trustee (Nos. 11/12), Mr Julian Byng (for the Straffords at No. 5) and Dr J. B. Robinson, who from the Arundel Castle Archives supplied such valuable sidelights on Norfolk House in the 'old days'.

Finally, the author would indeed be ungrateful if he did not acknowledge the generous enthusiasm of Mr Dennis Hill, Chairman of the St James's Square Trustees, who got the book off the ground in the first place and who has put such energy and imagination into it ever since.

D.M.F.

Note on Numbering and Street Names

The numbering of houses in St James's Square has been affected from time to time by the division or amalgamation of sites. There was also a major change in 1864 involving all houses from No. 8 onwards (p. 102).

Of the Square's tributary streets, York St was renamed as Duke of York St in 1937 and Charles St as Charles II St in 1939.

For the convenience of readers, modern numbering and nomenclature have been used throughout, except in one or two direct quotations.

Foreword

The Trustees of St James's Square, London, are extremely proud of their inheritance. For some 260 years, since the Act of Parliament was passed forming the Trust, they have been 'cleaning, adorning and beautifying' that 'Great Square Place or Piece of Ground called by the Name of Saint James's Square'.

It is therefore fitting that they should commission the present book, thus recording the events, people and buildings that establish this 'Piece of Ground' as one of the most famous areas in London.

Denys Forrest has undertaken an enormous task researching every corner of the Square and has produced a fascinating story which brings its history up to date. The only previous work on this subject was written in 1895 by Arthur Irwin Dasent, which in itself was a milestone and to which many references have been made in the text.

The author has also been guided by the Minute Books of the Trust, the early volumes of which have been deposited with the City of Westminster Library Archives Department. These Minute Books date back to the first meeting of the Trustees in 1726, when the list of names reads like an extract from *Debrett's Peerage*.

Today the private owners have gone, and all the Trustees represent Companies or Institutions with premises on the West, North or East sides of the Square, as the Act of 1726 stipulates.

On behalf of the Trustees, I do hope that the reader will enjoy this volume and become as enthusiastic as we are about the treasure that we inherit and continue to maintain and improve.

Chairman of the Trustees

1. *Henry Jermyn, 1st Earl of St Albans. After Van Dyck(?)*

I
The Bailiwick of St James

Among the rejoicing cavaliers who escorted King Charles II on his triumphant return from exile in the month of May 1660, none had fairer prospects than Henry Jermyn, newly created Earl of St Albans. The third son of a Suffolk landowner, Sir Thomas Jermyn, of Rushbrooke, he was already a courtier in the happiest days of Charles's father, having been appointed Vice-Chamberlain to Henrietta Maria within three years of her arrival in England in 1640 for her marriage to the King. Later he became her Master of the Horse. On the eve of the Civil War he was created Baron Jermyn and accompanied the Queen when, after playing a heroic part in the earlier stages of the struggle, she fled to France in advance of her husband's defeat and execution.

Once in Paris, Lord Jermyn seems to have dug in very comfortably. There are plenty of witnesses to the *grand luxe* in which he contrived to live while those about him could scarcely make ends meet—'. . . rolled to every entertainment in mid-winter Paris in his new coach,' as Carola Oman puts it, 'spattering noblemen of ancient lineage who had reduced themselves to penury in the royalist cause.'[1]

Nor was there much doubt that one reason for 'Harry Jermyn's' immunity from the shabbiness and indigence which was the rule in that circle was his intimate connection with the Queen Dowager. Indeed the rumour ran (as so often in such contexts) that she had secretly married him, and even that 'they had had a daughter between them in France'.[2] That seems unlikely, but the widow Queen was certainly dominated by her 'subject spouse', and this he turned crisply to account when the spoils of the Restoration were shared out.

2. *Sutton Nicholls's view of St James's Square (1st state,* c. *1722).*

Not least among them was the Bailiwick of St James. This was the name given to the extensive tract of meadowland originally put together by Henry VIII from the holdings of Westminster Abbey, the Convent of Abingdon and the Hospital of St James (on the site of St James's Palace). The Bailiwick lay mainly in the area now bounded on the east by the Haymarket, on the north by Piccadilly and on the west and south by the Royal Parks. At the Restoration it formed part of the Queen Dowager's jointure, with Lord St Albans as one of her trustees. However, as early as March 1661 he himself obtained a lease of the Bailiwick, due to run until 1691, followed quickly by something that proved even more valuable – the freehold of about half of the 45 acres of pasture known as St James's Field, the site in fact of the future St James's Square and its adjoining streets. He could now fulfil his ambition of creating a fashionable Court suburb, strategically placed between Westminster and the Palace of St James's.

There had already been some development at the eastern end of this area, and even before the Civil War part of the Field (hitherto used merely for grazing and occasional musters of royal troops) had been assigned to recreations such as a tennis court, a physic garden and a stately 'pall mall alley'[3] along the line of the present Pall Mall.

In contrast, the St Albans enterprise was to be a deliberate exercise in urbanism with, at the heart of it, a great residential *piazza* or square. There were precedents for both these terms, though they had been set well away to the eastwards. The Earl of Bedford's famous Covent Garden *piazza* dated from 1631–5, while Lord Southampton's Bloomsbury Square had only just been completed (first leases 1661). It is probable, however, that Lord St Albans was looking back rather to continental models for his ambitious project; he will have been very familiar with the Place Royale in Paris and perhaps with the Lyons Belle Cour, to which in fact visitors from France were accustomed to compare St James's Square.

St Albans seems to have begun his building operations within a year of Southampton's, even though his freehold only dated from April 1665, when it was issued to his two Trustees, Abraham Cowley the poet and Baptist ('Bab') May – hence the adjacent Babmaes Mews. Already towards the end of 1662 alarm bells had begun to ring in the City. Here is Samuel Pepys:

> November 21, 1662 . . . Going through the City, my Lord Mayor told me how the piller set up by Exeter house is only to show where the pipes of Water run to the City. And observed that this city is as well watered as any city in the world, and that the bringing the water to the City hath cost it, first and last, above £300,000; but by the new building, and the building of St James's by my Lord St Albans, which he is now about (and which the City stomach I perceive highly, but dare not oppose it) – were it now to be done it would not be done for a million of money.

Quoted so often without comment, this is in fact something of a puzzle. It is true that the City drew part of its water supplies from the vicinity of the River Tyburn at what is now Stratford Place, Oxford St, and that its pipes ran via

Conduit St to the eastern end of Piccadilly and thence along the line of the Strand. It is also true that the flow was often diminished by illicit 'quills' inserted en route, but his lordship of St Albans could hardly be suspected of plotting piracy of this kind to feed his grand houses.[4]

The latter were originally intended to be very grand indeed. St Albans wanted his square to contain not more than twelve or thirteen 'great and good houses, fitt for ye dwellings of Noble men and other Persons of Quality'. This again was probably an idea brought back from the Continent. But the British aristocrat, with a few spectacular exceptions, has never taken to the concept of a vast, free-standing town mansion, comparable to the *hôtels* of Paris or the *palazzi* of Venice or Rome. The family and social life of nobleman or wealthy squire was focussed on his country estates – all he needed in London was a convenient lodging for self, wife and daughters when they came up (reluctantly in his case) for the Season, and the type of 'terrace house' developed in the Carolean and early Georgian age seemed to fill the bill quite adequately. Mr C. S. Sykes' sumptuous volume, published as recently as 1985, may give a different impression, but of his sixty or so *Private Palaces*[5] in the West End of London, only about half were free-standing mansions; moreover, since he ranges in time over three centuries, not more than twenty of those were in existence (or at any rate in private occupation) at any one time.

Ultimately, then, twenty-three houses rose on the East, North and West sides of the new square – the South side, backing rather too closely on Pall Mall, was never properly developed and remained a problem and sometimes a nuisance until quite recent times (p. 26). As the plans on p. 9 show, the frontages in general ranged between 44 ft and 54 ft, the most prominent exceptions being mentioned below. The plots were deep enough (perhaps 200 ft on the average) to allow for quite decent gardens, as well as the stables and coach houses which were as essential as garages or parking spaces in the twentieth century. Only one St James's Square garden exists in recognizable form today, at No. 4 (p. 52); the last of the old stable yards, behind Nos. 5–7 and 10–12 for example, survived World War II, but can be seen no more.

How was Lord St Albans's scheme put through? He disposed of his plots to two main classes of buyers – fellow grandees in search of a modish address, and speculative builders. The latter usually bought on mortgage and either worked to the specification of a known client, or erected houses in 'carcase' form which could be finished off when a purchaser was found.

Conspicuous in the aristocratic segment were John, 1st Lord Balasye, who took over the largest site, 133 ft wide, at the southern corner of what is now Charles II St and comprising the present Nos. 32 and 33; Henry Bennet, 1st Lord Arlington,[6] and his brother John (later Lord Ossulston) with 110 ft on the north corner of the same street (Nos. 1 & 2); and George Savile, 1st Marquess of Halifax, with 80 ft at the corresponding angle of King St on the opposite side of the Square (Nos. 17[7] & 18). All men of family, but it will be observable throughout this chapter how many new creations were represented among the St James's Square peers. Lord St Albans himself settled at first for half of what is now the site of Norfolk House (No. 31), but in 1676, while the Square was still in the formative stage, set about building himself a great mansion on the North side where Chatham House, plus No. 11, stands today.

Even there, he did not long remain, because in 1682 the house was sold for £9000 to James Butler, 1st Duke of Ormonde. It would be impossible to pursue here the public career of the Crown's great servant in Ireland (the only man to be four times Lord-Lieutenant), or that of his less fortunate grandson and successor, the 2nd Duke;[8] we can but record that for the next thirty-three years under the name of Ormonde House, their mansion was the scene of a princely hospitality which was long remembered.

Ducal splendour continued even longer, though against a less securely aristocratic background. When Ormonde House came up for auction in April 1719, following the impeachment and exile of the 2nd Duke four years earlier, it was bought for £7500 by an Irish attorney called Hackett, who swiftly transferred it (at a comfortable profit of £2500) to the underbidder, James Brydges, 1st Duke of Chandos. Paymaster-General of the Forces in Marlborough's wars, when £15 million is supposed to have passed through his hands – who knows how much stuck to them? – Chandos is best remembered as the builder of glorious Canons, at Edgware, as the patron of Handel and as the alleged original of Pope's satiric portrait 'Timon'. We shall be hearing more of him.

The speculators were an interesting lot. Nicholas Barbon, for example, son of the notorious politician 'Praise-God Barebones' and one of the pioneers of the London terrace house – he built No. 4 and sold it (in contentious circumstances) to Antony Grey, 10th Earl of Kent. The names of Richard Frith, who bought several sites, including those of Nos. 14 and 15, Sir Thomas Clarges (No. 13) and Abraham Storey (No. 6) are still familiar on the map of London's West End. One family of developers no longer perpetuated in this way are the Angiers, though the alley behind the North side of the Square which now comprises Apple Tree Yard and Ormond Yard was originally named after them. It was the Angiers who built both No. 7, which they sold in 1677 to that expensive nobleman Richard Jones, Viscount (later Earl of) Ranelagh (p. 34), and No. 16. The latter they held onto until as late as 1785, when Burrage Angier and his daughter got £3500 for it from the Earl of Lichfield, who had ideas of enlarging No. 15 next door.

But whoever did the building, the original occupants of Lord St Albans's houses, and a long train of their successors, were overwhelmingly aristocratic. A few samples from the early days. No. 3 was erected by a Mr Shaw of Covent Garden, but was taken over by William, Lord Cavendish, son of the 3rd Earl of Devonshire and himself destined to be the 1st Duke. Subsequently there were short lets to a glittering shoal of tenants – the Earl of Ossory, the Duchess of Grafton, the Earl of Bridgwater, the Duke of Shrewsbury and the Earl of Carlisle.

At No. 5, both Abraham Storey and another speculator called Clisby were involved in the development, but the first name in the rate book is that of Henry Hyde, 2nd Earl of Clarendon. Then in 1684 the house was bought by Elizabeth, Countess of Thanet, whose husband had been executed by Cromwell. The Countess in turn let No. 5 to a very un-Irish-sounding Duke of Leinster, Meinhardt Schomberg (son of William's famous commander at the Battle of the Boyne), to be followed by Charles Lennox, 1st Duke of Richmond, the Duke of Shrewsbury (on transfer from No. 3) and, after a solitary commoner (Mr Edward Coke), Charles Beauclerk, 1st Duke of St Albans.

At the other end of the Square it was much the same picture. Of No. 13, tucked into the north-west corner, the Clarges family long retained the freehold, but their tenants in the early days included Lawrence Hyde, son of Lord Clarendon (No. 5) and future Earl of Rochester; at least three more incipient Earls, Richard, Lord Lumley (Earl of Scarbrough), Lord Conyers Darcy (Earl of Holdernesse), Francis, Viscount Newport (Earl of Bradford); and a brace of earls regnant, so to speak, Robert Spencer, 2nd of Sunderland, and No. 7's Lord Ranelagh (for a brief spell). An ambassadorial interlude (p. 20) followed, then two steps up in the peerage to George Fitzroy, 1st Duke of Northumberland.

No. 14, at right-angles to No. 13, was given the smallest frontage of any in the Square (27 ft), but soon it too acquired some high-sounding occupants. After Frith had sold it to Sir Fulke Lacy and the latter had passed it on to Sir John Williams of Minster Court, Thanet, we are well into Debrett once more. John Dawnay, 1st Viscount Downe, is succeeded by Lord Lumley (ex No. 13), John Vaughan, 3rd Earl of Carbery, the 3rd Lord Poulett and Ann Lady Crewe, with her third husband, Arthur Herbert, 1st Earl of Torrington.

We find No. 15 (another Frith speculation) again well garrisoned by the peerage, but we are also brought face to face with another element of high significance in our story – the mistresses of the Stuart Kings and their offspring. The Square itself, of course, had been a courtly enterprise, with the Queen Dowager's presumed lover as its impresario, and from the start these royal connections – on the wrong side of the blanket – came thick and fast. We have already had a passing brush with three of King Charles's bastards, all by different mothers – at No. 5, Charles Lennox, Duke of Richmond (by Louise de Kerouaille, Duchess of Portsmouth) and Charles Beauclerk, Duke of St Albans (by Nell Gwynn); at No. 13 George, Duke of Northumberland (by Barbara Palmer, of whom more shortly).

Confusingly, the famous Frances Teresa, Duchess of Richmond ('La Belle Stuart'), whose name stands first among the tenants of No. 15 (1778–9), had no connection with the aforesaid Charles Lennox, except that the King was collateral male heir to her husband, the 3rd and last Duke of Richmond and 6th of Lennox, of the old Scottish line. Frances and the Duke were married in 1667, but the Duke died only five years later at Elsinore, of all places, having been sent as ambassador to Denmark to get him out of the way. Charles probably came

3. Frances, Duchess of Richmond. Wissing & Van der Vaart.

nearer to being genuinely in love with Frances than with any other member of his seraglio, and indeed she must have been a charmer – can we forget Pepys's description of her 'with her hat cocked and a red plume, sweet eye, little roman nose and excellent *taille*'[9]? Frances long resisted the King, who in desperation thought at one time of trying to get a divorce and marrying her, but she is believed to have yielded in the end.

Not long after the Duchess of Richmond's brief tenancy of No. 15 ended in 1679, came John, 18th Earl of Kildare and his beautiful wife Elizabeth. She was the daughter of our acquaintance Lord Ranelagh, but Dasent leaves it in some doubt whether it was she or one of her unmarried sisters at No. 7 who 'attained the dignity of being numbered among the King's many mistresses'.

The mansion whose name linked it most directly with King Charles's entourage did not receive its royal seal of approval until the next century. Cleveland House (No. 19) began in fact as the residence of the Capels, Earls of Essex. The first of them, we may note in passing, suffered terribly while Lord-Lieutenant of Ireland (1672–77) from the financial demands of the 'female harpies' surrounding his Majesty, who regarded the Irish Exchequer as fair game. Not the least rapacious was Barbara Villiers, later Barbara Palmer, then Countess Castlemaine (when her husband was ennobled) and finally Countess of Southampton and Duchess of Cleveland in her own right. Her personal stamping-ground was that area of St James's which still has Cleveland Row at its heart, but in 1721 her son Charles, by then Earl and Duke, bought the old Capel home for £5000, and 'Cleveland House' it and its successors on the site have remained ever since.

Before deserting the ladies of King Charles for those of his brother James, we need to move southwards to the site of what used to be the last house in the SW corner of the Square. By modern numbering it would rank as 22, but that has been assigned elsewhere, so we have ventured to christen it '21a'. It stood alongside the present 20/21, but in 1847 it was demolished to provide an extended site for the Army & Navy Club (p. 110).

As with No. 3, the '21a' plot was granted by Lord St Albans to Edward Shaw of Covent Garden. In October 1673 the house he built on it was sold to 'Madam Davis', as the rate books courteously describe that 'impudent slut' of a dancer and singer, Moll Davis, who so shocked and delighted Samuel Pepys. Moll seems to have become the King's mistress in about 1669, and was at first accommodated in a house in Suffolk St. Her daughter by the King, known as 'Lady Mary Tudor', eventually married the 2nd Earl of Derwentwater and thus became the mother of the unfortunate young Jacobite Earl who perished on Tower Hill in 1716.

The reign of Moll Davis at '21a' lasted until 1688, when the house appears to have been bought by Lord Ossulston, of No. 1; its subsequent history does not concern us at the moment.

It will be seen that the legend linking this house with Nell Gwynn is without

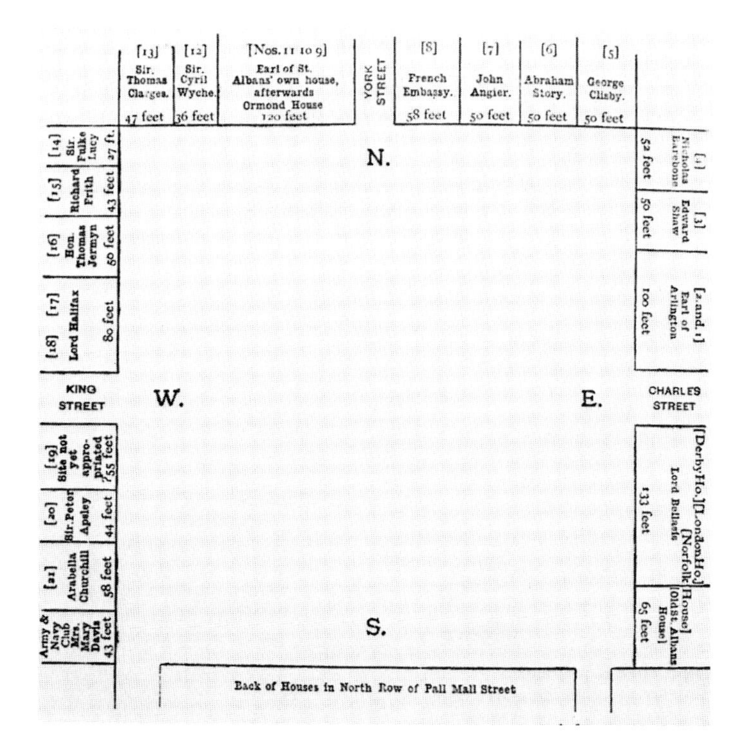

4. *Allocation of building sites in the Square, 1676.*

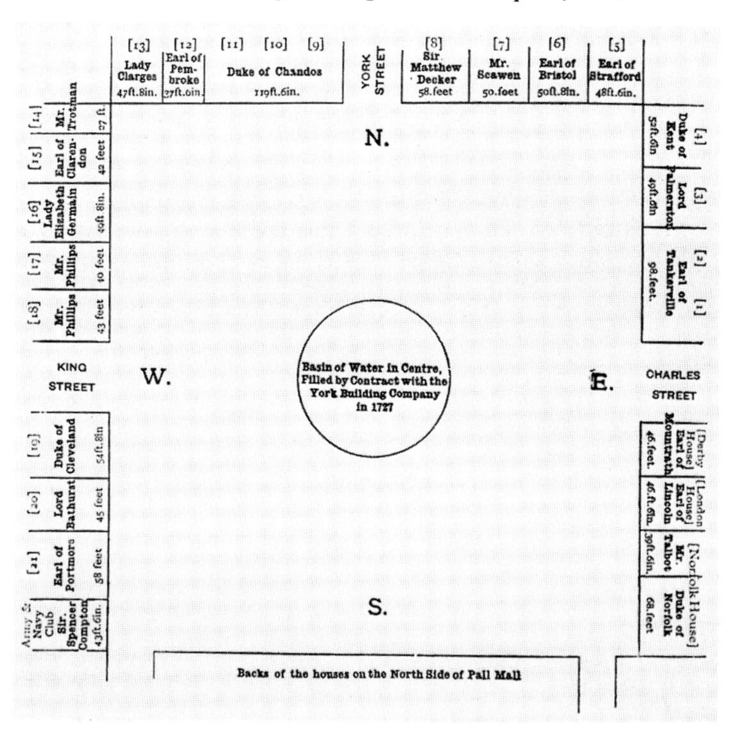

4a. *The Square at the passing of the Improvement Act of 1726.*

foundation – the nearest she came to St James's Square was an address on the south side of Pall Mall opposite the Army & Navy Club. But we did meet her son Charles, 1st Duke of St Albans (no relation of the Jermyn Earl) at No. 5, and much later the 8th and 9th Dukes will be found at No. 21 next door to Moll Davis's old home.

Long before that, this very house was identified with both of the best-known mistresses of James II – Arabella Churchill and Katherine Sedley. No. 21 was in fact built for the former, with whom the Duke of York (as he then was) is supposed to have fallen in love when she was Maid of Honour to his Duchess and he was teaching her to ride. She was only seventeen at the time, but she quickly saw to it that her even younger brother John was given the first step on the ladder which would lead him to immortal glory as the Duke of Marlborough.

Arabella occupied No. 21 from 1675 until 1678, when the Duke of York's favour was transferred to Katherine, daughter of that notorious Restoration rake, Sir Charles Sedley.[10] No. 21 was then let, though it would seem that Arabella's husband, Colonel Godfrey, retained an interest in it.

On February 6 1685 King Charles died and was succeeded by his brother. At this point King James's advisers felt that the Sedley connection was indecorous, so the King reluctantly dismissed Katherine, doubling her allowance and buying No. 21 as a replacement for her lodgings at Whitehall. But the lovers continued to meet on the quiet, and in January 1686 Katherine was created Baroness Darlington and Countess of Dorchester. Despite the Glorious Revolution of 1688 and King James's exile, she lived on at No. 21 until in 1696 she married Sir David Colyear, a strapping one-eyed soldier of fortune who had served in the Dutch Army and had come home to England in the train of William of Orange. Within three years of his marriage he was created Baron Portmore (later Earl), at which point he and his wife made a temporary exit from St James's Square.[11]

While King William himself was considered to favour his own rather than the opposite sex, even he had a *maîtresse en titre*, Elizabeth Villiers, Countess of Orkney, and it is almost a surprise to find that she did not, as far as we can trace, ever make her nest in St James's Square. Notice must be taken, however, of at least one clandestine offshoot of the House of Orange, even though the personage concerned, Sir John Germain, did not move into No. 16 until 1705. His 'official' father was a private soldier in the Dutch regiment of Life Guards, but his mother is believed to have been the mistress of William II of Orange and he himself dropped significant hints in his coat-of-arms.

Not long after Germain came to England in the train of his putative half-brother, William III, he made himself notorious by his liaison with the wife of the 7th Duke of Norfolk, which culminated (after several spectacular false starts) with a divorce in 1700. They then married, and when the ex-Duchess died in 1706 she left Sir John a huge fortune. The following year he married Elizabeth, daughter of the 2nd Earl of Berkeley. He himself survived until the year 1718, but after that Lady Betty (as she was universally known) settled down to an

5. *Katherine Sedley, Countess of Dorchester. Studio of Lely.*

immensely protracted widowhood which embraced not only endless routs and card parties at and around No. 16, but the friendship of men of letters such as Pope, Swift and Horace Walpole. She also became respectable – 'outlived the irregularities of her youth', as one observer put it.

Lady Betty died at No. 16 in 1769, leaving her money to Lord George Sackville, a younger son of the Duke of Dorset. He came into the picture because he had married a daughter of old Sir John's close friend and comrade-in-arms, Lieut-General William Colyear, of the Portmore family (above). Lord George (who then took the name of Germain) was an active politician, but as Colonial Secretary during the American War of Independence, endured nearly as much 'flack' as he had as Lord George Sackville at the Battle of Minden in 1759.

We must now devote a little space to some appendages of St James's Square, and to the later days of the family which provided them.

II
The Last of the Jermyns

Lord St Albans's vision for his new and splendid suburb was not confined to the demure quadrangle of three- or four-storey brick mansions, with pilasters of the same material and modest stone dressings as their sole adornment. Like any twentieth-century 'developer', he aimed to attract the right sort of occupants by providing them with amenities. These included a Market – equivalent to the modern shopping precinct – and a Church, for which a social centre is more likely to be substituted today.

St James's Market was apparently a spacious, H-shaped structure lying athwart the course of the future Lower Regent St. It was described in 1720 as a 'large place with a commodious Market house in the midst, filled with Butchers' Shambles, besides the stalls in the Marketplace, for Country Butchers, Higglers and the like'. At the SW corner was a paved alley, giving access to Charles II St and thence into St James's Square. It is amusing to note that provisions were reckoned to be 25 per cent dearer than in the equivalent markets in the City, whence in fact they were brought for resale to 'the Stewards of the People of Quality, who spare no price to furnish their Lords' Houses with what is nice and delicate'.[1]

Following the Regent St development from 1815 onwards, the Market was moved a little further east – the present St Albans St and Norris St roughly mark the site. The last traces of the Market were removed soon after World War I.

The first impulse towards the building of Wren's famous Church of St James's Piccadilly came from the local inhabitants, who petitioned the House of Commons in April 1664 that the Bailiwick should be constituted a new parish, carved out of St Martin-in-the-Fields. But the legislation which ultimately went through six years later was referred to as 'the Earl of St Albans' Bill', and there is no doubt that he paid for the greater part of the structure. It is only fair, therefore, that the Jermyn coat-of-arms (p. 13) should still appear on the keystone over the west door of the tower.

As local government by parish 'Vestries' grew in importance up to the middle of the nineteenth century, this was a highly important turning-point in the history of St James's Square. We do not propose, however, to attempt a description of the Church itself, in which Wren took so much pride and which was restored with such faithfulness by Sir Albert Richardson after the tower and roof had been destroyed and the superb interior gutted by bombs in World War II. There are two reasons for this.

In the first place, it is curious that, considering its origins, the Church was never integrated architecturally into the layout of St James's Square. Sited between Piccadilly and Jermyn St, its east–west orientation might have made this difficult, but the genius of Sir Christopher Wren could surely have contrived for the tower and steeple to form a terminal feature at the end of Duke of York St. Instead, there was a rather half-hearted substitute in the form of a big, pillared doorway at a mid-way point along the south aisle (visible on pp. 2 and 15). Even this was swept away during alterations in 1856.

In the second place, though St James's Church was from the start extremely fashionable, and attendance during the London season almost a *sine qua non* for the grand families of the Square (and even at times for members of the royal family from further afield), hardly any of them are commemorated within its walls. All that pomp of gilded marble was reserved for the parish churches nearest to their country seats (or, in exceptional cases, for Westminster Abbey or St Paul's) – another indication of the Square as a seasonal roost rather than a *home*. This is the more striking since, as we shall see, the ownership of a number of the houses has shown a continuity which may be familiar in the shires but is extremely rare, if not unique, in a residential quarter of the capital. In spite of generations of Legges, for example, maintaining their London base at No. 1, Boscawens at No. 2, de Greys at No. 4, Byngs at No. 5, Herveys at No. 6, Ansons at No. 15, Howards at No. 31 (Norfolk House), the only member of any of these tribes with a tablet in St James's Church would seem to be Anne Boscawen, niece of the famous admiral (south aisle). And as for the Square's seventeenth-century Williamite grandees, their sole representative is the King's friend and firework impresario, Henry Sidney, Earl of Romney (p. 19), and even he is banished to the gallery (north side).

Apart from the coat-of-arms already mentioned, the Jermyns are not to be found there either. One cannot avoid the thought that they are more aptly commemorated by the name of the rather worldly thoroughfare which cuts off the Church from Duke of York St and the Square. They were a raffish lot. Writers like Evelyn positively revel in taking Lord St Albans apart; in youth with a physique which 'gave him credit for manliness which he did not possess', in old

6. *St James's Church, Piccadilly. By J. Coney, 1814.*

age gambling on and on until he could no longer see the cards and someone sitting behind him had to count the pips – 'a loathsome monument to decayed debauchery'.

When he died at last in 1684 he left no heir and his earldom became extinct, but by special remainder his Jermyn barony devolved in turn on his two nephews Thomas and Henry (Lord Dover). Thomas had a son, but he met a tragic end:

> Thursday December 29 1692. Last Tuesday Mr. Jermin, of ten years of age, son and heir to the Lord Jermin and nephew to the Lord Dover, being on a lighter in the Thames near Beaufort Steps, the wind blowing very hard bore down the mast which fell on his head and broke his skull, of which blow he died within an hour. He was the only male heir to the family of Jermyn and Dover, whose estates are said to be worth £30,000 per annum.[2]

When Thomas, Lord Jermyn, himself died in 1705 he was succeeded for a few years by his brother Henry, created Baron Dover in 1685 and Earl in 1689 – Henry, the 'little Jermyn', notorious as a duellist and a womanizer and one of the many lovers of Lady Castlemaine. From then onwards the Jermyn estates were dispersed among a variety of female co-heirs. However, a St James's Square family which can claim descent from two of them are the Herveys, Earls and later Marquesses of Bristol, whose tenure of No. 5 from 1677 until as recently as 1955 was the longest of any in the Square. The story is a trifle complicated, but the main elements are:

> 1. Abraham Storey, who built the first house on the site, sold it in 1676 to John Hervey, Treasurer of the Household to Queen Catherine of Braganza and 'the honest founder of our family', as he was described by his nephew and heir. This was another John, later Lord Hervey and 1st Earl of Bristol, whose grandmother Susan was the daughter of Sir Robert Jermyn, then squire of Rushbrooke.
>
> 2. The second link is through Mary, Lord Jermyn's second daughter and co-heiress, married to Sir Robert Davers, 2nd bart. of Rougham. Their grand-daughter Elizabeth, sister and heiress of Sir Jermyn Davers, 4th bart., married (1752) Frederick Hervey, the celebrated 4th Earl and Bishop of Derry,[3] and took part of the old Jermyn estates with her.

In view of all this, and the fact that he eventually inherited Rushbrooke itself, the 5th Earl and 1st Marquess no doubt felt justified in taking 'Earl Jermyn' for his subsidiary title when receiving his step in the peerage in 1827.

Apart from these somewhat fine-drawn links with No. 5, the Jermyns retained two significant holdings in the Square, but not for very long. The Earl of St Albans continued to live in his great house on the North side of the Square until December 1682 when he sold it to the Duke of Ormonde. Facing this mansion on the opposite corner of Duke of York St stood No. 8. The *Survey of London* describes this as 'the last house in the Square to be granted away by the representatives of the St Albans interest, being owned by the Earl's heirs until

1721'. The first mention of it is in 1676, after which it was usually let, the tenants including two French Ambassadors – Honoré Courtin (1676–77) and Paul Barillon (1686–88). Between them came Sir Cyril Wyche and the 8th Earl of Pembroke; however there must have been an interlude of Jermyn occupation during 1684, because it was on July 13th of that year that Henry Compton, Bishop of London, appeared there to receive from Lord Jermyn's representative the title deeds of the St James's Church site, and carry them in solemn procession up Duke of York St. and into the Church. What is slightly surprising to read is that he returned to No. 8 for refreshments halfway through the consecration ceremonies.

Four years later, Jermyn's brother, Henry, Lord Dover, moved into No. 8 and remained until 1693. Lettings were then resumed, only terminating with the sale of the house to a City man, Sir Mathew Decker, in 1721.

However, the last lingering vestige of the old Jermyn interest in St James's Square today relates to none of the above houses. That privilege is reserved for No. 16. Ever since the Angier family built it in 1676 on a site granted by Lord St Albans to his nephew Thomas, the house carried a rentcharge of £15 8*s* 6*d* for the benefit of a tiny almshouse near the Jermyn seat of Rushbrooke in Suffolk. This represented about half the total income of what was known as Lord Jermyn's Charity, whereby four 'almspersons' – two old men and two old women – were housed, clothed and fed.

Not unnaturally, successive occupants of No. 16 have always felt fairly numb and vague about the Rushbrooke almshouse, and the story, at any rate from the nineteenth century onwards, has been of considerable periods of arrears, belated solicitors' letters and denials of all knowledge by owners or tenants. The most recent instance was in 1978, when the East India Club suddenly received a claim for nine years' rentcharge. After some correspondence (in which Lord Rothschild, the current owner of Rushbrooke, became involved), payment was resumed. By then, the number of almspersons had been reduced to two; it is understood that the almshouse has since been closed, and the charity continued in another form.[4]

III

'The Great Square Place'

Even if it did not exactly run to palaces, the new Square provided a tiptop 'address', and behind its dignified façades the full-blooded social life of the late seventeenth century could be carried on with panache. There was only one drawback, and that must have been obvious whenever an aspiring hostess glanced through her drawing-room windows. All she could observe until her eye travelled to the far side of the Square, was a large, rough open space – featureless, it would seem, except for a shed about 30 feet long, impudently erected by a coach-builder for the storage of his timber. Otherwise, nothing but piles of offal, rubbish, cinders and the occasional dead dog or cat.

If there was any action to be seen, it may well have been in the form of crude proletarian sports, judging at least by a curious paragraph in the *Evening Post* for March 28 1731. This recorded the committal to prison of a certain William Bellamy (alias Vinegar) whose father formerly 'kept the ring in St James's Square for cudgel-playing'. One would like to know more!

However, there was one periodic exception to this otherwise drab scene. After the Restoration, firework displays became a fashionable form of public rejoicing, and for these St James's Square – 'the great square place', as the original grant to Lord St Albans[1] called it – was the favourite arena. Much of it was still in the builders' hands when one of its most important mansions, St Albans House (on the site of the future Norfolk House) was lent to an unusual visitor from abroad. This was Cosmo de Medici, Hereditary Prince of Tuscany, usually known by his eventual title of Cosmo III. He had been sent on a European tour by his father, the Grand Duke Ferdinand II, in order to escape the imbroglio of what had turned out to be a disastrous marriage to a French Princess, daughter of Gaston of Orléans.[2]

The Prince arrived in London in the spring of 1669, and the story of his adventures here is told respectfully but with spirit by a member of his suite, Count Lorenzo Magalotti.[3] From the Count's narrative we learn with what flattering politeness his master was received by the Court and noblesse of Britain, and the rich impressions he gathered, not least at Oxford and Cambridge. Lord St Albans's house was his headquarters throughout, and the King's birthday occurring when he was just about to leave in early August, he decided that he ought to manifest some 'special tokens of joy'. Accordingly he caused to be constructed in front of the house

> a machine with fanciful artificial fire-works and squibs which, as far as the shortness of the time and the skill of the artist permitted, were well contrived.

The populace assembled in droves, revelling in the spectacle, and particularly in the casks of Italian wine and beer which were broached, the applause being seconded by 'discharges of harquebuses and carbines' let off by members of the Prince's suite.

Contrary to what has been sometimes stated, King Charles did not attend this pyrotechnic extravaganza (he may have seen it reflected in the night sky over Whitehall or St James's), but a couple of evenings later he very condescendingly came to supper. The preparations were terrific, even the knives and forks being arranged in a 'fanciful and delicate manner'. Seventeen gentlemen sat down to an array of eighty magnificent dishes;[4] many more stood around. The climax of the feast was an excellent course of confectionery, but scarcely was it set upon the table when it was carried off and plundered by the people who had come to watch the show. Not even the presence of the King – to say nothing of his carabineers – was enough to prevent the pillage of these 'very delicate viands'; one wonders whether His Majesty was used to such exhibitions of the national manners.

King Charles certainly watched fireworks in the Square some twelve years later, when he dined with the French Ambassador, M. Barillon, at No. 8. This was a very stately affair, in honour of the birth of a son to the then Dauphin (August 1682).

However, the Square did not reach its apogee in that particular respect until the arrival of Henry Sidney, Earl of Romney, as the occupant of No. 16 (1691–1704). Among the seven dignitaries who invited William of Orange to England in 1688, he held one high office after another. Yet he was alleged to have been 'drunk once a day for many years', a terror to husbands and according to Swift (who had a personal grudge), 'without any sense of truth or honour'. More relevant from our point of view is that as Master of the Ordnance, Romney was well placed to play with gunpowder on a royal scale. Nor was that the whole story. Serving under him was Sir Martin Beckmann, a Swedish artillery officer who had been a captain in the British Navy and took an important part in both the construction and the demolition of the famous Tangier mole. In 1685 he was knighted and became Chief Engineer and Master Gunner in the Ordnance Department. Fireworks seem to have been his hobby, and two designs almost certainly by him are still to be found in the library of his friend Samuel Pepys at Magdalene College, Cambridge.[5]

One was for the splendid celebration of the capture of Namur (August 4 1695) to which Romney invited the King. Evelyn[6] describes this as 'famous fireworks and very chargeable' and says the King's Guards encompassed the Square, as Lens's mezzotint indeed shows.[7]

Two years later, Romney and Beckman were in action again, this time to mark the Peace of Ryswick – December 2 1697 (p. 18). And what a conflagration they provided!

1000 Skyrockets (of 4–6 lbs weight) — 400 Light balls
200 Balloons — 15,000 Swarms
2400 Pumps with stars — 7000 Reports
1000 Cones

22 rocket chests each containing 40 rockets from 1 to 4 pounders

No wonder the performance is said to have cost some £10,000, though Dasent quotes a correspondent of Viscount Hatton as saying that it was not worth anything like that – worse still, several people were killed by falling rocket sticks, one of which created panic when it crashed through the roof of Halifax House (No. 18).

Even this wild scene, however, can hardly have outshone the rival fiesta staged by Heer van Citters, the Dutch Ambassador, on October 27, the day appointed by the States-General as a thanksgiving for the Peace. This took the form of a 'very noble bonfire' erected in front of No. 13 and consisting of 140 tar-barrels placed pyramid-wise on seven scaffolds and kindled to the sound of trumpets, while the inevitable hogsheads of wine were broached. It seems fortunate that No. 13 remained unsinged.

That was not quite the end of the story – as late as February 24 1715 Peter Wentworth[8] writes (apropos of the Peace with France) 'there's fireworks making which is to be in St James's Square' – but the days of pyrotechnic megalomania were over. This was partly, no doubt, because of the damage caused by Sir Martin Beckmann's recklessness, but also because they became the occasion of dangerous squib-throwing. It is Luttrell who tells us that several persons were taken up for this and that one victim was none other than Lord Jermyn, the 'squire' of St James's Square, 'having one thrown in his face 'tis said put his eye out and will endanger the other, if not his life, being in a fever'.[9] He survived, but the Lord Mayor and Aldermen (though not directly concerned, of course, with

7. Firework display in the Square for the Taking of Namur, September 1695. B. Lens.

the Square) published an Order, forbidding the making, selling and throwing of squibs, and offering a 10*s* reward for any information laid.

In any case, the time was not far distant when the St James's Square residents would decide that it was up to them to set what we would nowadays call their 'environment' in better order. On February 25 1726 a Petition was presented to the House of Commons, stating that the Square

> had lain and doth lie rude and in great disorder, contrary to the design of King Charles II, who granted the soil for the erecting of capital buildings on the East, West and North parts thereon.

The petitioners (their names have not come down to us, but no doubt they were all or some of those listed in the subsequent Act) were willing to contribute 'in a rateable proportion' to putting the Square to rights, but they could not do so without an Act. The Chancellor of the Exchequer here chipped in to say that His Majesty gave his consent so far as his interest was concerned.

The proceedings which followed throw a surprising light on the speed with which private legislation could be pushed through a crowded parliamentary programme in the earlier days of Sir Robert Walpole.

The Petition was immediately referred to a Committee which was ordered to hold its first session at five o'clock that same evening in the Speaker's Chamber.

A week later (March 2), the Chairman, Charles Montague, reported back. He announced that they had heard three witnesses – Messrs Wm Hargreave, Charles Hunt and Wm Benny. All had deposed that they had known the Square for many years, and that 'the same hath lain, and does lie, in a filthy condition and as a common Dunghill', with loads of ashes and rubbish deposited on it by the inhabitants and that 'cats and dogs had likewise been cast upon the scene'. There was also the story of the coachbuilder and his shed.

So who were they, these public-spirited deponents, who helped so efficiently to make up the committee's mind for it? Well, we do not know anything more about Wm Hargreave, but Charles Hunt and Wm Benny were a few months later appointed Receiver and Clerk respectively to the Trustees of St James's Square!

Leave was duly granted for a Bill to be brought in, and within another five days (March 7) it had been drafted, presented to the House and given its second reading.

Four days more and it was passed to a large and powerful committee, two members of which, Mr Byng and Sir Theodore Wentworth, might well be supposed to have had an interest in the prospects of No. 5 St James's Square. Again, the direction was for a meeting that evening in the Speaker's Chamber, and within 24 hours the committee had reported, with various amendments. These were agreed, as was the sole Lords' amendment, which inserted 'or the major part of them' after 'Trustees' at one point. On April 26, Royal Assent was received.

Now to the Act itself (Cap. XXV, Anno Duodecimo Georgii Regis). The preamble, having rehearsed the 'rude, waste and uncleanly state of the Square', as already familiar to us, puts forward the desire of the inhabitants on the East, North and West sides to 'clean, repair, adorn and beautify the same', by raising an adequate contribution by and amongst themselves. This the Act authorizes them to do, and goes on to appoint the following as the first Trustees:

The Most Noble Duke of Norfolk, Earl Marshal
Charles, Duke of Cleveland
Henry, Duke of Kent
James, Duke of Chandos
The Rt Honourable Thomas, Earl of Pembroke
Henry, Earl of Lincoln
Henry, Earl of Clarendon
David, Earl of Portmore
Thomas, Earl of Strafford
Charles, Earl of Tankerville
John, Earl of Bristol
The Rt Honourable Algernon, Earl of Montrath in the Kingdom of Ireland
Henry, Lord Viscount Palmerston in the Kingdom of Ireland
The Rt Honourable Sir Spencer Compton, Knight of the Bath
Sir Mathew Decker, Baronet
Thomas Scawen, Samuel Trotman and George Clarges, Esquires

A list like that – headed by four Dukes and stiff with Whig peers – might well help to explain the speed with which the whole exercise had whizzed through. Whether the Bill's 26 Clauses would have benefited with more leisurely vetting is at least open to question.

In broad principle, the Trustees were authorized to 'clean, repair and otherwise adorn' the Square; to prevent as well as to remove 'all manner of Annoyances by Filth, Dung, Ashes, Rubbish or otherwise'; and also to remove existing encroachments and to prevent new ones. On the other hand, in contrast to the Petition's reference to King Charles's grant of the soil, there is no mention of *ownership*. Trouble stored up for the future, as we shall see! Nor is a right to enclose any part of the central area even hinted at.

In matters of detail, too, the Act shows sign of hasty drafting. The Trustees' essential power to levy Rates is limited to 'ten shillings a Foot for the front line of the said Houses . . . on the above-mentioned East, North and West sides of the Square' without any provision to increase this should emergency or a change in the value of money demand it. The result is that from that day to this the utmost limit of the Trustees' Statutory Rate income, on 1216 ft of frontage, has remained at precisely £608.

Anomalously, the possibility that the Rate would not be sufficient to pay for the beautification programme was recognized (in ponderous detail) in Clauses XVII–XXII inclusive, which permitted the Trustees to raise up to £6000 from the residents by the sale of annuities.

There is also a curious lack of foresight in the Act's pedantic provisions for the routine of meetings. The Trustees are to assemble for the first time 'at the Vestry Room of the said Parish of St James's on the 21st day of April in the year of our Lord one thousand seven hundred and twenty six', and thereafter on the third Thursday of every April – stipulations which were ignored in year 1 and in almost every subsequent year of the Trust's existence. A quorum for the initial meeting was to be five, out of the eighteen founder Trustees; yet later clauses named seven as the quorum to fix the Rate, three for any intermediate meetings, seven to consider complaints about assessment or to appoint a Receiver of Monies, and 'the major part of them' (that Lords' amendment!) to authorize the transfer of annuities or to appoint new Trustees.

And who exactly were the latter? Initially of course the gentlemen listed above, comprising in fact the owners or tenants of every occupied house in the Square except No. 16 (Lady Betty Germain, excluded as a female), but thereafter vacancies were to be filled by co-option; nothing was laid down as to whether owners or occupiers were *entitled* to trusteeship, which in fact (Clause XXIV) reverted to the Trust whenever anyone alienated his title in his house. Here again, a blurred situation in the future could be foreseen.

As to enforcement, the Trustees were (and presumably are) entitled to distrain on the goods of anyone failing to pay his or her Rate and, in the event of the 'rescous or tortious taking away' of goods so distrained, to recover treble damages and costs by court action (Clause XIII). They were also authorized to haul before the Justices any depositors of filth who, on conviction, would have to pay the Trust 20*s*; encroachers might have to pay up to £50. A minor sanction (Clause V) was that any coachman standing or plying for hire in the Square should forfeit 10*s* – all he was entitled to do was to deposit his fare, and depart.

The final provision (Clause XXVI) was that although promoted by the residents, this was now 'deemed and taken as a public Act' and all Judges and Justices were required to take note of it accordingly.

Such was the famous St James's Square Act of 1726, the first of its kind ever passed to regulate a London square, and apparently the only one to remain in operation, unamended, to the present day. Next in point of age were the Lincoln's Inn Act (1735), Red Lion Square (1736), Charterhouse Square (1742), Golden Square (1750), Berkeley Square (1766) and Grosvenor Square (1774). All these, and a score of other promoted subsequently, have either been drastically amended or have passed into oblivion through Local Authority take-overs, or by default.

As we shall see, the powers actually exercised by the St James's Square Trustees have progressively diminished, even though the Act has remained unchanged, and as far as we can trace those powers have never actually been challenged in the courts. It is not without interest that in one parallel instance at least, Portman Square, the freehold of which is still owned by the Portman Family Settled Estates, the validity of the Acts (1782 and 1833) governing its gardens has been recognized as 'at least questionable'. This is partly because the surrounding properties no longer provide 'householders' as defined in the Acts, and Deeds of Variation have been entered into with individual lessees for the levying of a Rate.[10] It is perhaps fortunate that 'householders' do not figure in the St James's Square Act.

Certainly, on any strict interpretation, the Trustees were *ultra vires* from the start. Their first meeting took place on June 23 instead of April 21 1726, and though on that occasion ten Trustees attended, in scarcely any subsequent year until very recent times were the statutory seven present to agree the Rate. However, in the late nineteenth century a fairly consistent effort was made to collect additional signatures retrospectively!

The Rate fixed at this inaugural meeting was 2*s* 6*d* per foot of frontage. Otherwise the main business was to appoint the already mentioned Wm Benny senr as Clerk at a salary of £30 per annum and Charles Hunt as Receiver, and to commission a certain Thomas Ackres[11] to make a general survey of the Square, marking off the length of each frontage and noting down encroachments. The most significant minute, however, is the final one:

> The Commissioners[12] dǫ not conclude whether the sd Square shall be inclosed, or open by levelling or paving, till they have a report of the expences both ways.

No misgivings, it will be observed, about their *powers* to enclose the Square if they so wished.

In their first year (though very seldom since) the Trustees did not confine themselves to an AGM, but held further meetings in July, August and November. At the July meeting, apart from signing the Rate, they ordered

Anno Duodecimo

Georgii Regis.

An Act to enable the preſent and future Inhabitants of the Eaſt, North, and Weſt Sides or Lines of Saint *James's* *Square*, to make a Rate on themſelves for raiſing Money ſufficient to clean, adorn, and beautify the ſaid Square, and to continue the ſame in repair.

HEREAS a great Square Place or Piece of Ground called by the name of Saint James's Square, in the Pariſh of Saint James Weſtminſter, encompaſſed on the Eaſt, North, and Weſt Parts thereof, with Principal or Capital Buildings, and on the South Part by the Back of the North Row of Houſes in Pall Mall Street, doth now lie, and hath for ſome Years paſt lain rude, waſte, uncleanly, and in great diſorder, and Incroachments are made thereon: And whereas many of the ſaid Inhabitants of the ſaid Houſes on the Eaſt, North and Weſt Parts of the ſaid Square are alſo Owners and Proprietors of ſuch Houſes, and they and the reſt of the ſaid Inhabitants are much diſſatisfied with the ill Condition of the ſaid Square, and are deſirous to clean, repair, adorn, and beautify the ſame, in a becoming and graceful

Preamble.

Sffff 2

B

8. *The Act of 1726 (detail of first page).*

Ackres to 'take a level' of the Square and to compute the number of loads of rubbish etc. therein; we never hear the result, but no less than 3792 cubic yds of surface soil had to be removed in the following year, when the centre was being drastically replanned. On August 3 the Trustees received a report of an encroachment of 2 ft on the Square in respect of two houses owned by 'Mr Phillips'[13] and on November 11 William Benny was instructed to write letters to the Commissioners of the Waterworks of Chelsea, the New River and York Buildings. The importance of this move will appear in the next chapter.

The South Side

As architecturally planned and as legally embodied, St James's Square consisted of the West, North and East sides only, the South being looked upon as no more than the 'backside' of the corresponding range in Pall Mall. The original intention was to bisect it with quite a wide thoroughfare equivalent to Duke of York St, instead of narrow access roads (John St and the now obliterated George St) at the east and west ends respectively.

In any case, the fact that there was and is only 60 ft of depth between Pall Mall and the Square would always have made a double row of dignified residences impracticable. Nevertheless, a few small structures soon began to front the Square, and from time to time one or two of them even exhibited shop signs.

Against such intrusions the Trustees waged a constant war. More than that, they insisted from the start that even the Pall Mall residents had no right of communication through to the Square except after 'proper application' to themselves and in accordance with any restrictions they chose to impose. Bow windows, areas, coal-shoots and garden gates were all regarded as 'encroachments'; in a typical instance (April 17 1766), the well-known Pall Mall bookseller, Andrew Miller, asked to be allowed to dig vaults and an area to an agreed distance under the Square, and was only given permission on payment of 2*s* 6*d* rental per foot of frontage.

One of the few structures on the South side which seems to have gained some acceptance as part of the Square was Adair House at the west end. In the same year as the Miller petition, 'Mr Adair' was mulcted of £4 13*s* 9*d* in respect of his area and bow window, but because a later member of the family subscribed to the John Nash improvements of 1819 (p. 84), his successors applied for and usually obtained keys to the Garden. Later still, Adair House became a branch of the War Office and as such was a target for Fenian outrage (p. 124); its eventual fate was to be sold for a handsome sum ('not far short of £60,000', according to Dasent) to make way for the extension of the Junior Carlton Club in 1885.

Meanwhile, in spite of constant suggestions that the South side should be cleared completely, and even opened up to Pall Mall,[14] a more or less continuous row of small houses sprang up, and by 1819 we shall find the occupants being

9. No. 31a St James's Square, enlarged from a three-storey terraced house of 1770.

graciously permitted to pave and light the footway in front of their residences at their own expense. Several of them, however, were no more than lodging-house keepers, and in Knight's *London*[15] of 1843 the author remembers 'a whole detachment of the Irish parliamentary brigade' having its quarters there. By then, the South side houses had their own numbering, 1 to 10, leaving Adair House in solitary grandeur as 'No. 1 George St', but from about 1860 onwards they were incorporated into the general numbering of the Square.

Two surviving small Georgian houses (Nos. 23 and 24) perished in the blitz, and today much of the South side does little more than provide massive rear façades to office blocks, whose main entrances are in Pall Mall. Happily, this does not deter several of the occupants from identifying with the Square and subscribing to the upkeep of its garden.

A final note: Some impression of what the old South side may have looked like can still be gained from that quaint survival (now numbered 31a) just south of Norfolk House, where the Arundel estate had its office at one time. Originally an extremely modest terrace house of about 1770, on three floors only, it had a couple of extra storeys piled on top in Victorian times. A fragment of the original Norfolk House railings, complete with Ns and ducal coronets, survives in the angle between No. 31a and No. 31 (p. 54).

IV

A Basin and a Statue

Up to the end of 1726, the 'beautification' campaign had not got very far, as recorded in the Trustees' Minutes. It is not until the meeting held on February 7 1727 (attendance 10) that the crucial decision is taken: the Square is to be open, without posts or rails 'except about the intended bason'. The latter is to be 'sunk to the level of ye Pavement', 150 ft in diameter and 4 ft deep, and to be encircled with an octagonal iron-work at 10 ft distance and 5 ft high. This iron-work 'to be joyned to 8 stone Obelisks to carry lamps'. Estimates to be brought in by Mr Bridgeman for 'what had been resolved to be done', and anything else needed to finish the Square.

The 'bason' may have been 'intended', but this is its first appearance in the Minutes. Yet, remarkably enough, the genesis of it goes back beyond that letter of November 11 1726 to the three waterworks companies – even beyond the setting up of the St James's Square Trust. In the Huntington Library, California, where rests the correspondence of James Brydges, 1st Duke of Chandos, is to be found one really surprising communication. It is addressed by His Grace to a certain Capt. Burroughs, is dated March 12 1726 and reads as follows:

> There is to be on Monday evening a meeting at the Duke of Norfolk's of the Inhabitants of St James's Square to consider the best method of beautifying the Square.
>
> So that if you intend to speak to them on behalf of York Buildings Co. I believe it will be advisable to see as many of

> them as you can before that time. I have already spoke to Lord Pembroke, Ld. Lincoln and Sir Mathew Decker, and Lord Carnarvon [Chandos' son] intends to endeavour to ingage Lord Montrath in your favour. These will concur, I am apt to think, to accept your Proposals, and no time should be lost in applying to ye rest.

In other words 'beautification' was being discussed in detail while St James's Square Bill was still in Committee of the House of Commons, and at least one prospective Trustee was already canvassing like mad!

To make sense of this situation, we need to recall that though Chandos had only moved into his grand house in 1720, within four years he was already thinking of moving out again. This was partly because of losses in the South Sea Bubble, but also because his interest was now concentrated on Cavendish Square and particularly on the reservoir there and other waterworks with which he was involved. He had recently become chairman of the York Buildings Company, which since the reign of Charles II had been taking water from the Thames at a site roughly at the bottom of Villiers St, Strand. He saw no reason why some of this water, pumped up by the York Buildings 'fire engine',[1] should not profitably be sold to the residents of St James's Square, and even had it at the back of his rather cloudy mind that the basin might come in useful, perhaps as a sort of relay station.

It may well be asked how an ornamental pool in the middle of a square could possibly serve such a purpose. But Chandos seems to have had similar designs on Bloomsbury and other squares, and his editor, Collins Baker, chides Dasent for failing to recognize the utilitarian purpose of the 'reservoir'. Moreover, the urgency with which Chandos set up his canvass in March 1726 and his optimistic belief that perhaps he owned the central area himself, could hardly have been stimulated merely by the prospect of being allowed to keep the basin filled. The remarkable size and depth of the latter also has to be taken into account. Would a sheet of water at least 4 ft deep[2] and with a capacity of about 440,000 gallons (or nearly 2000 tons) ever have been mooted unless the person behind it had some such operation in mind? And why, for that matter, should the Trustees have stipulated (Minute of February 6 1767) that not more than 6 ins. of water should be drawn off at a time?

In the early stages, however, the affair proceeded on an overtly competitive basis. The New River Company does not seem to have responded to the Trustees' letter of November 1726, but at the meeting on February 7 sealed bids from York Buildings and Chelsea were opened and were further considered on February 22, when a strong posse of Trustees assembled, headed by all four Dukes (Norfolk, Cleveland, Kent and Chandos). The sequel was that on March 2 a sub-committee was appointed to 'draw up proper heads and to treat with the Commissioners of York Buildings, whose proposals are the best made yet'. We discover without surprise that the first name on the sub-committee list

10. *James Brydges, 1st Duke of Chandos. By Van der Myn.*

11. *Sutton Nicholls's view of St James's Square (2nd state* c. *1727–28).*

is that of the Duke of Chandos, his colleagues being Lords Palmerston, Strafford and Bathurst, Sir Mathew Decker and Mr Scawen.

Everything, no doubt, had been cosily settled in advance and the basin never figures again until May 1742, when the New Company of York Buildings,[3] is allowed £15 per annum for keeping it full. No mention of using it as a 'reservoir', of course – the Duke had long since vanished from St James's Square, taking his dreamy imaginings with him, and the very fabric of Chandos House had been sold for demolition (1735). In 1748, the New River Company managed to grab the contract, undercutting York Buildings by £5.

York Buildings had nothing to do with the general layout of the central area. That was entrusted to Charles Bridgeman, first of the long line of landscapists, gardeners and nurserymen who had been recruited to plan and replan those few acres. It could indeed be claimed that Bridgeman came first in rank as well as time. As Royal Gardener, he had two Kings, George I and II, as his clients and for them he created the Serpentine and Kensington Gardens; privately, he advised Lady Suffolk at Marble Hill, Twickenham, Lord Oxford at Wimpole and Lord Carlisle at Castle Howard, and was in close touch with at least one Trustee, Lord Bathurst.

In the Square, however, his task was minimal and certainly involved no 'gardening' as we know it. The scheme for which he had been asked to provide estimates at that February 7 meeting consisted of no more than the circular basin, the gravel walk, the octagonal railing and the extensive area of paving outside. The second state of Sutton Nicholls's engraving conveys the scene. Each of the eight obelisks had a stone stump at its base to 'keep off the coaches', and the paving of the Square itself was carried out by a character referred to as 'Mr Mist the pavior'. Purbeck flags – 'square cubick stones commonly called French paving' – were used, and added vastly to the prestige of the Square. The Basin itself was given a bed of solid flints, set in clay, as excavations in 1985 were to reveal.

Bridgeman received £5630 under his contract (less £510 – the value of the old paving-stones), out of which substantial sum he presumably had to pay Mr Mist and other 'tradesmen'.

* * *

To the casual eye, the Trustees' main duty to the Square had now been completed, but one feature – though long foreshadowed – was still missing. Luttrell assures that as early as December 1697 (in the midst of the fireworks era) the King's statue in brass was 'ordered to be sett up in St James's Square, with several mottoes and devices, trampling down popery, breaking the chains of bondage, slavery etc.'[4] A fine flamboyant idea, and we must regret that not even a sketch for it survives. From then onwards, the story is one of quite extraordinary frustration, over a full century.

The next appearance of the phantom statue comes in the will (signed in 1711) of Richard Jones, 1st Earl of Ranelagh. A resident of six years in the Square,[5] Ranelagh is one of those deplorable characters whom one can never quite bring oneself to deplore. Witty, devious and extremely fat, he started life as a pupil of John Milton, but somehow graduated to being Chancellor of the Exchequer for Ireland (1668–74). In that post of vantage he managed to misappropriate some £76,000, yet when William of Orange came in, the King not only remitted any penalty, but in 1691 made Ranelagh a Privy Councillor and appointed him – of all people – Paymaster-General of the Forces.

12. Solid flint bed of basin, as exposed in 1985.

Predictably, he now set a precedent for his successor, the Duke of Chandos, by enriching himself to the extent of a further £72,000. After twelve years of plunder, he resigned rather than face an enquiry; this time it was Queen Anne's turn to refuse to prosecute. In old age Ranelagh devoted himself to the beautiful house west of London which gave its name to Ranelagh Gardens. He died in 1712.

Ranelagh's will is typical of the man. Its final clause provides that if no private debts remain and if nothing is outstanding on his public accounts ('after my equitable demands, the most considerable of which I have set out in my own hand in the little book which I commonly carry in my waistcoat pockett'), plus a few other contingencies, anything left over is to be applied to

> erecting in St James' Square the statue of my dear master King William on Horseback in Brass, in case the same be not then erected.

Needless to say, nothing came of this. The next fiasco was in 1721, when according to Malcolm,[6] the Chevalier de David tried to raise a subscription for a St James's Square statue to be sculptured by himself. Only this time the subject was to be King George I – more topical perhaps, but not necessarily more popular among all those Whig grandees. 'The Chevalier de David' means Claud David, a Burgundian and alleged pupil of Bernini, who had come over to England with ambitious ideas about public commissions. He did get a royal order for a couple of statues somewhere in the precincts of St James's Palace, but nobody wanted his George I – a mere £100 was subscribed – and his only identifiable monument today is the rather impressive one to Philip Carteret in the North Aisle of Westminster Abbey.[7]

And so we arrive at the name of Samuel Travers, MP. A Treasury official under Godolphin, he was for a short time Surveyor-General of the Queen's Lands (as Wren was of Buildings) and also served as Surveyor-General for the construction of Blenheim Palace. He made a will which curiously echoed Ranelagh's, providing for a statue in St James's Square or at Cheapside Conduit 'to the glorious memory of my Master King William the Third'. Travers died in October 1725, and on March 16 1727 the Trustees (aware no doubt of past history) asked one of their number, Lord Palmerston, to 'apply to the executors of S. Travers Esq. in relation to the late King William's statue'.

What ensued was another very long pause, broken only by a marginal scribble in the Minutes of April 12 1753: 'Memo to speak to Mr Car(e)y [an executor] about King William's statue.' The fact was that Travers's will had been contested. Not until November 1767 were Letters of Administration granted to the Governors of Christ's Hospital, the residuary legatees. Then silence once more, but there must have been a stirring of the waters, because on April 17 1794, nearly three-quarters of a century since the testator's death, the St James's Square Trustees called a special meeting for the 30th of that month 'for the purpose of settling the business of the statue'. And at last we have a formal Minute:

> April 30 1794. The Trustees present at the Board, having taken the opinion of several absent Trustees respecting the erection of the statue of the late King William III, find a majority of them in concurrence with themselves now present, and are for having the same placed in St James's Square. Ordered that Mr. Saunders (Clerk) write to Mr. Moberley to inform him that the Trustees (care being taken that the water is not injured) do assent to erecting the statue.

The tempo remained as leisurely as ever, and it was only on April 6 of the following year that 'Mr. Moberley and Mr. Bacon' attended a meeting of Trustees. The former was now described as 'Agent' for Christ's Hospital – he was in fact their solicitor – while the latter must have been the sculptor John Bacon snr, who had apparently already shown sketches to a select group of Trust members. This time, as a body, the Trustees were decidedly cagey, emphasizing that they were only 'suffering' the statue to be erected, and were in no way responsible for any expense whatever attending the same. A lot more Tories in

13. John Bacon snr. Painting by William Bates.

the Square by then, and maybe the whole idea of commemorating King William was *vieux jeu* . . .

In point of fact, considerable vagueness still surrounds the actual commissioning, execution and erection of the statue, though some light is thrown by an Indenture of February 4 1804, preserved among the archives of Christ's Hospital, now lodged in the Guildhall Library.[8] The signatories are Richard Corp, on behalf of the Governors, and John Bacon jnr. Here is recorded the transfer of the job from Bacon's father, after his death in 1799, and the obligation of the young man to complete the statue (along with 'a proper pedestal and other requirements'), 'according to the model in plaister of Paris now prepared for casting in bronze, which said model was partly prepared by the late John Bacon and since his decease finished by John Bacon the signatory and now in his possession, and also in accordance with a drawing'.

Elsewhere, the Indenture records an advance of £1500 against a total estimated cost of £5000, though a marginal note to another document mentions £3275 3*s* 9*d* as the actual cost.

According to Mr Gunnis,[9] a third member of the Bacon family, young John's less well-known elder brother, Thomas, may have lent a helping hand. Casting

14. William III. Designed by John Bacon snr and executed by his son, 1805–7.

in bronze is said to have been carried out at the Bacons' Newman St premises – not too well, if later events are any guide. Characteristically, the statue now disappears again from the Trust Minutes for nearly twenty years – all we know from outside sources, is that it was 'erecting' in July 1808, and there was certainly no unveiling ceremony, such as we might expect in 1986.

What did it stand on? Obviously the stately pedestal of today, with its fine bronze lettering

GVLIELMUS III

on each long face and, on the east side only, carved in smaller type, I. BACON, IVN^r, SCVLPT^r. 1807. Some people, however, even Pevsner, have been under the impression that the pedestal had stood there empty since the date of Travers's will. But in the early days at least the centrepiece of the basin was a fountain or *jet d'eau*. ('The Lords expect the fountain will play so many hours a day' – Minute of May, 1727.) The fountain in turn was surrounded by a low plinth – perhaps designed already with the statue in mind. At some stage the fountain ceased to operate and about 1778 the plinth itself seems to have been removed, to the annoyance of a gentleman having 'some interest in the ducks', which no doubt nested or sunbathed on it.[10]

Anyway, pedestal, horse and rider must have looked very fine, reflected in the great pool, and very fine they look today, even without anti-papal mottoes and symbolic devices. A pleasing thought, surely, that James II, unhorsed outside the National Gallery, should share with his mounted supplanter the flattering convention of Roman armour. James is elegant enough, thanks to the genius of Grinling Gibbons, but William has the advantage of his sweeping cloak and the superbly modelled tail and mane of his steed. If only the two monarchs could confront each other in St James's Square!

William's horse, it will be observed, has its near hind hoof slightly raised. By tradition the mound supporting it represents the molehill with which the 'little gentleman in velvet' encompassed the King's death. The present writer, like many before him, has been guilty of repeating this,[11] but he now suspects nothing more than a baroque device to give the limb 'movement'.

All in all, a splendid seventeenth-century conception, brought to late but triumphant birth.

V

The Architects Move In

At the time of the passing of the 1726 Act and perhaps for a quarter of a century following, the outward aspect of St James's Square changed very little. There had been occasional reconstructions – we remember how at an early meeting the Trustees noted encroachments by 'Mr Phillips', builder of two houses (Nos. 17 & 18) on the site of the old Halifax House at the northern corner of King St. Some time before 1725 this mansion, reported to be 'in visible danger of falling', had been sold for £6500 to John Henry Mettins, a London jeweller. The Savile (Halifax) family tried to buy it back, but in the end it passed to a carpenter, Thomas Phillips, of the parish of St George's, Hanover Square. He demolished it, but the notable thing is that the houses which he substituted were strictly in what might be called the 'Lord St Albans manner' – red or brown brick, four storeys high (including dormers) and four windows wide, the windows being linked by slight stone dressings.

Much the same thing happened when three houses were erected in the 1730s on the site of the great mansion called in turn St Albans House, Ormonde House and Chandos House.

Lord St Albans's Square in fact provided a Carolean pre-existence for what we nowadays regard as the Georgian style, surviving examples of which are to be seen by the thousand from Highgate to Streatham, Islington to Richmond. It is a style which has established an unshakable hold on the affections of twentieth-century connoisseurs of the London scene; we look back with puzzlement at the reaction of Tennyson and his contemporaries against what they regarded as its drab and deadly monotony ('*the long unlovely street*'). Usually one regards this as an essentially Victorian feeling, but criticism of plain brick facades in the fashionable quarters of London goes back much further.

In the year 1771 appeared a 70-page pamphlet which may have attracted little attention at the time, but which in several respects hinted at changes of direction in our story. Entitled *Critical Observations on the Buildings and Improvements of London*, it was issued anonymously by Dodsley of Pall Mall, but from a very early period, and on convincing grounds, has been attributed to James ('Athenian') Stuart, architect of the present No. 15 St James's Square.

Claiming the right of every individual to 'discuss with decent freedom the merits and demerits of public works and even private undertakings as far as they related to public ornament', the author uses a brisk and sometimes satiric pen to put forward his own ideas.

We shall be adverting later to one of his principal butts, the layout of London squares, but are here concerned with the other, the design of façades. Discussing the 'street house' – terrace house in our own day – he marvels that the nobleman whose proud country seat is adorned with all the riches of architecture, porticoes and columns, should be contented in town with a simple dwelling, convenient no doubt within, but unornamented without. Pardonable perhaps in a residence merely rented for the season, but not in a family mansion, where we expect something more than 'the mere requisites of a packer or sugar broker'. The Square itself provides his much-quoted instance:

> Would any foreigner, beholding an insipid length of wall broken by regular rows of windows, in St James's Square, ever figure from thence the residence of the first duke of England? All the blood of all the Howards can never ennoble Norfolk House.

This of course refers to No. 31 as rebuilt by Brettingham for the 9th Duke (Chap. VI). The façade can be seen on the right of Bowles' 1752 view of the Square (dust jacket).

A couple of pages later we reach what is no doubt the pay-off passage in the *Critical Observations* as a whole. After insisting that a unity of order enriched with ornament, in fair and highly polished materials, is what seems to be required, Stuart (for it is surely he) goes on:

> Nor are models of this sort wanting among us. The two houses lately erected by Mr Tufnell, in Cavendish Square[1], are fine examples; as is also that of Mr. Anson, in St James's Square. When once this last is completed according to the plan, the public will be more able to do justice to the classic taste which directed it. In its present state, it is wonderfully beautiful, and will serve to convey what is here meant . . . The expense of adorning a front can never be an object of consideration with a man of high rank . . .

Truly the Puff Audacious! And it must be admitted that the pillared façade of No. 15, as designed for the Anson family by Athenian Stuart himself, is an enduring monument to the 'classic taste' of the architect.

Was his panegyric also intended as 'bait' for further commissions to convert the prosaic brick fronts of the St James's Square mansions into imitations of ancient Greece? If so, it did not succeed so far as he personally was concerned, but we are soon to see his colleagues and rivals marching down that road.

But first, a word about one or two earlier rebuilding schemes which involved architects of note, without affecting materially the elevations of the Square. In December 1725 took place the only serious St James's Square fire (to date), and it was long remembered. It broke out in No. 4, then occupied by Henry Grey, 1st Duke of Kent – otherwise known as 'the Bug' – who had received his dukedom from Queen Anne as compensation for giving up his place as Lord Chamberlain (bought from Sarah, Duchess of Marlborough for '10,000 pieces'). No. 4 was burnt to the ground, in spite of the efforts of the insurance companies' firemen and of a detachment of foot guards hurried thither by the Prince of Wales (the future George II) in person, to fight the blaze and to prevent looting. Frantic, and finally successful, measures to save the adjoining No. 5 were conducted with some acrimony, as Peter Wentworth reported to his brother Lord Strafford.

The rebuilding of No. 4 followed quickly, and from time to time distinguished names have been attached to it. Dasent, for example, believed that Lord Burlington took a hand; Nicholas Hawksmoor is known to have prepared drawings; while Giacomo Leoni has been brought into the picture on the strength of certain phrases in an essay on building which he presented to the Duke. The *Survey* finds nothing characteristic of the work of any of these maestros in the typically 'St James's Square' facade of No. 4, as we see it today.[2]

Curiously enough, the famous fire has left us with a tangible link between Hawksmoor and the then No. 3, though that house has of course disappeared. Its predecessor, built by Edward Shaw (p. 5), showed signs of collapse in 1711, and reconstruction began the following year. Just how far Hawksmoor became involved with the owner, Lord Ashburnham, we do not know, but the *Survey* points out (Vol. XXIX, p. 84) that after the fire his colleague, Sir John Vanbrugh, commented to Lord Carlisle that No. 3 'did not receive one shilling's worth of damage, nor was it found necessary so much as to remove any goods. This is due to the advice Mr Hawksmoor and I gave to my Lord Ashburnham at the building of it'. An advertisement by the Sun Fire Office rubbed in the point.

Other architects who were employed on early- or mid-eighteenth-century rebuilding schemes were the Palladian, Henry Flitcroft, and the Brettinghams, grandfather and grandson. Flitcroft played an indistinct part in the design of Nos. 9, 10 and 11, the three houses which replaced the Duke of Chandos's mansion, while in addition to the Brettinghams' involvement with Norfolk House and No. 21 – to be described in Chapter VI – Matthew Brettingham snr rebuilt No. 5 in 1748/9 for the 2nd Earl of Strafford. His façade probably looked rather more 'St James's Square' than the present grand Palladian refacing in stone by Messrs Cubitt (1854).

It is possible that Brettingham was wholly or partly responsible for the rebuilding of No. 13, though not for the exterior painting scheme which deceived even Sir John Summerson[3] into believing that the façade was composed entirely of grey 'headers'. He certainly submitted plans for No. 15 before James Stuart entered the scene.

* * *

And so we come to the 1760s and what may be called the 'Stuart revolution'. Constructed in fine Portland stone instead of brick, the pillared and pedimented frontispiece of his No. 15 had its origins in the drawings and measurements which he made when he travelled to Greece with Nicholas Rivett. These he embodied in his grand folio *The Antiquities of Athens* (1762), which virtually introduced this country to the formulae of Greek architecture. No. 15 was his first work in the new style, apart from one or two interiors, and can be regarded as a manifesto.

The house previously on the site (p. 6) had come into the hands of the Anson family when the 1st Lord Anson, the great Admiral, bought it from the 4th Earl of Clarendon. Anson died in 1762, leaving No. 15 to his elder brother Thomas, a bachelor and a connoisseur who, as the *Survey* suggests, may have made James Stuart's acquaintance through that convivial body, the Society of Dilettantes. By 1763 the old house had been pulled down and within three years its successor had been designed, built and occupied. Correspondence between Stuart and Anson shows the pride which the former took in the job and the personal care which, for example, he gave to the execution of the capitals of the four Ionic pillars which articulate the façade, and which he had derived from the Temple of Minerva Polias (part of the Erectheum).

What we need to realize is that Stuart's No. 15, a small masterpiece in its own right (opposite), disrupted the harmony of St James's Square as decisively as any development of the past fifty years. His pamphlet shows no consciousness that if his example were to be followed by other architects and their clients, the result would be not 'a unity of order enriched with ornament', but strident competition between one facade and the next. We do not have to wait long for proof. In the very year in which the *Critical Observations* appeared, a second St James's Square connoisseur began to take steps towards replacing what he doubtless regarded as his obsolete mansion. This was the fabulously wealthy North Wales baronet, Sir Watkin Williams Wynn, who had acquired No. 20 from the Bathursts. His first choice as architect seems to have been James Gandon (better known in Dublin), who actually produced plans, but having taken a look at the glories of Osterley Park and Syon House, Sir Watkin followed fashion and hired the brothers Adam.[4]

In its way the façade of No. 20 (now of course duplicated by No. 21) is as masterly as No. 15, though it shows a very different approach to the classical style. It is extremely rich, but because there is no pediment, and flat corinthian pilasters are substituted for Stuart's engaged columns, the challenge to the prevailing reticence of the Square must have seemed less strident (p. 71). The

15. In this nineteenth-century engraving, 'Athenian' Stuart's No. 15 façade (still almost unchanged) is flanked (left) by part of No. 16 and (right) No. 14, before they were rebuilt in 1864 and 1896–98 respectively. The provenance of the engraving is uncertain, but judging by the condition of No. 14 ('the worst house in the Square'), its sources almost certainly predate the acquisition of the house by the London Library in 1845.

job was finished early in 1775, and May Day could be celebrated with a 'musical breakfast' (whatever that was) and dancing below stairs.

The Adam brothers were now in full cry. Robert had been mainly responsible for No. 20, but it was John who in July 1774 wrote to Sir Rowland Winn, 5th baronet, of Nostell Priory in Yorkshire, offering him two alternative designs for a new façade to No. 11, which he had acquired in 1766. Robert had already stuccoed the existing front, but now the proposition was either for something quite plain which could be done for a mere £180, or a design with 'pilasters and corresponding ornaments' which might cost more than £500 but which would be 'as pretty as anything in the Square'. Either would be carried out in 'Mr Liardet's stonepaste'. Using a now-debased epithet, Sir Rowland chose the 'gay front', which was accordingly put in hand without delay. By February 1776 it was completed, and Robert Adam was able to report to Sir Rowland that 'every creature admires your front, and Sir Watkin told me the Square was much obliged to you, as it was a great ornament to the whole inhabitants'.[5]

Very civil of Sir Watkin, though it is difficult wholly to share his opinion. The 'pilasters and corresponding ornaments' of No. 11 (p. 47) strike one today as a rather gauche piece of *appliqué*, rather than as a fully integrated design like No. 15 or No. 20. This may be partly because some of the 'ornaments' have disappeared, including a decorative band between the first- and second-floor windows and a row of paterae (small roundels) above the pilasters. Even as completed, however, No. 11 can have been no *chef d'oeuvre*.

These three houses represent the visible legacy which the architectural efflorescence of the late eighteenth century has bequeathed to St James's Square. By a slight extension, however, one might include No. 32, executed in 1819–21 for the Bishop of London by the Cockerells, father and son, with its three elegantly recessed Venetian windows. Nothing important from the period seems to have been lost, in spite of the occurrence in the annals of such names as those of Henry Holland jnr (No. 7), his father-in-law 'Capability' Brown (No. 3) and Henry Holland snr (No. 8).

It is another matter, however, with what one may call the 'ghost houses' – ambitious schemes which were never executed, but for which quite detailed drawings have survived. The *Survey* illustrates two, either of which, had it been carried out, would have been a further affront to the St James's Square style.

One of these again involved Robert Adam. In 1772 No. 14 was bought by a retired merchant, Sir William Mayne. Four years later he was created Lord Newhaven, and no doubt by way of celebration, he invited Adam to give No. 14 a new face. The job was complicated by the narrowness of the frontage (27 ft, as previously noted). Adam sought to get over this by providing only two windows per storey (venetian at first-floor level), but inserting between them elaborate vertical panels adorned with candelabra and vase motifs. It is not known why the scheme never got off the ground.

No. 6 would have been even more of a surprise packet, had any of the ideas of George Dance jnr[6] been adopted. Called in by the 5th Earl (1st Marquess) of Bristol in about 1815, he prepared a whole series of designs, now preserved in the Soane Museum. All show a resolute breaking away from the normal 'terrace house' formula. One of them (*Survey*, Vol. XXX, Pl. 194a) is organized in three bays, but with only two windows per storey above the ground floor, the bay between being blind, except that the attic stage has three lunettes. These are divided into three lights by very thin verticals and the main windows (tall and rigidly rectangular) are treated in the same manner. Inconspicuous corinthian pilasters frame the windows, and the main decorative feature is a large-size Bristol coat-of-arms at second-floor level. There is something elusively 'modern' about all this.

One name still missing is that of Sir John Soane. Though we have described him elsewhere as 'the Square's favourite house doctor', nothing actually by him ever formed part of the St James's Square panorama. The nearest he got was some fairly drastic remodelling of the back parts of Robert Adam's No. 33

16. Robert Adam, architect of No. 20 and other works in the Square. Attrib. G. Willison.

(including the still visible Charles II St return) for Lord Eliot, later Earl of St Germans, who had bought it from the Earl of Buckinghamshire in 1805. One way or another, Soane was tinkering with this job (which led for a time to ill-tempered exchanges about the Bishop of London's stables next door) for nearly 18 years. Otherwise, the Soane involvement with St James's Square can be summarized as follows:

No. 3: Surveys and plans for the Earl of Hardwicke (1800, 1805) and subsequent works not affecting the façade.
No. 13: Painting of the exterior supervised for the Dowager Lady Ravensworth (about 1784).
No. 18: Surveyed in 1805 for his future client at No. 33, Lord Eliot. His advice – the price asked, £7000, was 'enormous'. No deal.
No. 21: For Soane/Brettingham complications, see Chap. V.

Both at No. 13 and No. 21, Soane seems to have been mainly concerned with interior planning and decoration for which, as his surviving works show, he had an original and impressive flair. And this is a reminder that so far our survey of the eighteenth/early nineteenth-century architects' impact on St James's Square has only been, as it were, skin deep. Nothing has been said about their interiors, a few of which are among the most important remaining from the period.

* * *

It can be assumed that the original St James's Square houses had been put together by the carpenters or bricklayers who contracted for them with no particular plan in mind – perhaps (in the idiom of Lady Wentworth – p. 55) just 'thre large rooms forward and two little ons backward' and that was that. But by the time James Stuart, and particularly the Adam brothers, took over, a different ethos prevailed. It has been stated in magisterial form by Sir John Summerson. Remarking that with No. 20 St James's Square, No. 20 Portman Square, Chandos House (near Cavendish Square) and No. 23 Grosvenor Square (now demolished), Robert Adam reached 'the highest point of imagination and artistry in the handling of the London house', he emphasizes that such designs are not

> a simple aggregate of well-proportioned and convenient boxes, but a harmony in which many contrasts reside . . . It is all devised for the conduct of an elaborate social parade . . not built for domestic but for public life – a life of continual entertaining in drawing-rooms and ante-rooms and 'eating-rooms', where conversation would not be wholly ephemeral, but where a sentence might be delivered which would echo round political England . . .
>
> Adam . . . ponders the assembly of the guests, the conversation before dinner, the procession to the dining-room; he considers where the upper servants stand, how the under-servants shall perform their duties without being noticed; and behind the parade he plans the easy privacy of lord and lady, with study, dressing rooms, closets and bed-chambers . . .[7]

This is surely the epitome of life as it was intended to be lived in our Square, at the height of its glory.

Sir John goes on, however, to remark that when that life died, the glory died with it. However lovingly preserved its décor, the Adam sequence of rooms

17. Façade of No. 11, as designed by Robert Adam, 1774. *18. Façade of No. 11 today.*

necessarily loses much of its meaning when adapted for the use of institutions, businesses or clubs.

Yet in one case at least, No. 20 St James's Square, it is still possible to make a worthwhile comparison of Robert Adam's actual plans (p. 48) with what survives today. The Entrance Hall, where a finely lettered lead plaque (rescued from the basement) records the building of 'Sir W:Wms:Wynn's House'; the pillared eating-room, and beyond it the music room with its splendid decorations by Antonio Zucchi and Nathaniel Dance; then the suite of smaller and progressively more private rooms, by which Adam always set such store – Sir Watkin's library, followed by his dressing- and powdering-rooms, whence, if the fancy took him, the famous Master of Foxhounds could slip through a rear passage to make sure that all was in order in the fourteen-stall stable and coachhouses.

Back then to the staircase hall and the grand stairs, so sumptuously though unexpectedly adorned with Theodore Ramos's copy of Raphael's 'Transfiguration'; this was commissioned in 1981 to take the place of the eighteenth-century one which did not survive removal and storage during World War II. At first-floor level, the two withdrawing-rooms repeat the layout below, but provide if anything a heightened idea of the Adam decorative style, above all in the elegantly curved ceiling of the second withdrawing-room, where the panels of classical scenes are again by Zucchi. Lady Wynn was given a suite approximating to her husband's, but with a large and extremely pretty dressing-room (carefully restored after bomb damage) taking the place of his library, and a bedchamber beyond (colour plate 2). Everywhere are chimney-pieces and mirrors of the finest quality, all designed in the Adam brothers' office, as is the door furniture and innumerable other details.

There have been losses, of course, notably the finely decorated laundry block and screen wall at the rear, which were deliberately scenic. But one can still feel

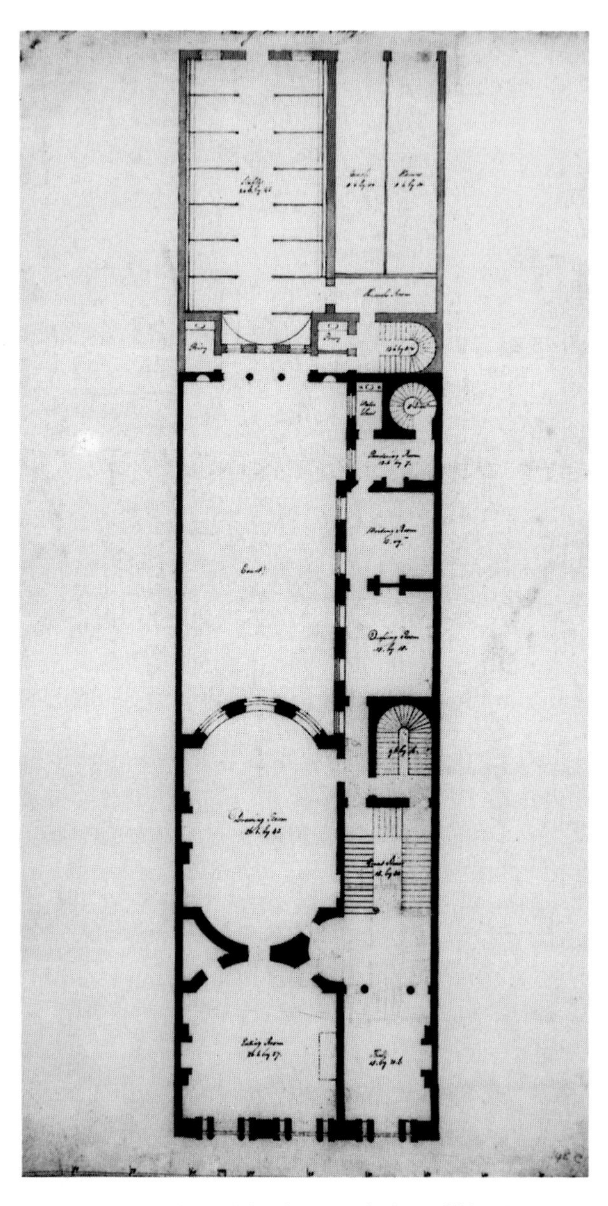

19. Robert Adam's ground-plan of No. 20.

20. Sir John Soane, a favourite house 'doctor'. By John Jackson.

that, with desks and conference tables magicked away, No. 20 could instantly reassume the role which Robert Adam planned for it, when he sat down to design 'one of the finest and indeed grandest town houses ever built'[8] – and all within a frontage of no more than 46 ft.

Next to Adam's No. 20, the most complete eighteenth-century interior still gracing the Square is undoubtedly that of No. 15, though the story is obscured by the decision in 1791 of the Anson of the day (Thomas, later Viscount Anson) to call in Samuel Wyatt to provide fairly elaborate embellishments. Samuel, an elder brother of the great James, was in strictly architectural terms among the less brilliant members of the Wyatt clan, but here he shows a distinct decorative talent, assimilating his motifs to those of that cool classicist, James Stuart, so that it is something of a specialist job to establish which of them did what.

There is also the complication of internal changes since the Clerical, Medical and General Life Assurance Society took over the house in 1856 (p. 100). The most notable of these was perhaps the removal of the grand staircase and the wide stone balconies above it, and their replacement by what has now become a large rectangular waiting-area. When this was first mooted in 1927, it cause considerable tremors and even the consultant architects, Messrs Curtis Green, had their doubts. It was not long before a round-robin reached the directors from ten senior staff members protesting against plans which they believed would 'irreparably damage a fine work of art in which they take great pride' – a display of sensitivity by the rank-and-file perhaps unique in such a context. However, the alteration proved a real *coup de théâtre*, since it opened up a spectacular view of the dome topping the staircase hall – it is uncertain whether its decoration, which includes four grand eagles with outstretched wings, is by Stuart or Wyatt (colour plate 1).

Otherwise, perhaps the best of the rooms remaining more or less untouched is the former principal drawing-room, occupying the whole first-floor frontage. It has benefited from Wyatt's only important alteration to the façade, when he lowered the sills of the windows to floor level. The great feature of this room, however, is the ceiling, where a shallow dome is supported by two octagons, one inside the other, and between them panels of classical mythology painted by Biagio Rebecca (12 gns a time for the large ovals, 5 for the smaller rectangles). There is more Rebecca in the former second drawing-room at the back, where Samuel Wyatt made the dubious insertion of a bow window. As at No. 20, most of the surviving Stuart/Wyatt rooms have lovely chimneypieces in the classical taste.[9]

Elsewhere in the Square, one receives only fragmentary impressions. Relics of the pre- and post-Adam eras intermingle, and both are too often overlaid by nineteenth- and twentieth-century afterthoughts. If we start at No. 4 (Nos. 1–3 having been completely rebuilt), we at once encounter this problem in acute form. The grand corinthian arcade through which one approaches the staircase hall, though of uncertain date, is known to be merely a latish substitute for a solid wall with a door in it; on the other hand, the staircase itself, with its niche enshrining a statue of Inigo Jones,[10] appears to be a genuine legacy from whoever reconstructed No. 4 after the fire of 1725. For the rest, we have a jigsaw of walls, ceilings and chimneypieces, partly original, partly pastiche; Lord de Grey (1834–59) may have been responsible for this feature, Lord and Lady Astor (1912–48) for that, yet the overall impression is of a great house cherished and aggrandized by a succession of private owners and worthier, even today, of a more sympathetic function than to house industrial tribunals (p. 157).

Among the earlier modifications, however, there is at least one which must also be regretted. This is the rear wing which partially obscures the charming little pedimented structure at the end of the garden or courtyard – all that is left to us of such features which were once almost universal in St James's Square.

At No. 5 next door (late Libyan People's Bureau), the *Survey* describes the interior of Brettingham's house as surviving with 'remarkably little alteration', so we have at least the bones of a mid-eighteenth-century design. But, though it was

21. Staircase of No. 4, possibly by Edward Shepherd. Statue of Inigo Jones from the workshop of Rysbrack.

quite carefully restored in the sixties, the decorative features have of course been a good deal knocked about since, and it has not been possible to verify how much of value is still visible.

No more survivals until Nos. 9 and 10. Just to what extent their interiors were from the hand of Henry Flitcroft remains as vague as his responsibility for the façades. Both have fine staircases of 1730s vintage, that of No. 10 being particularly stately, and a few ground-floor rooms retain that atmosphere too, but much else has been blurred by the adaptation of the two houses as the Institute of International Affairs.

The third house on this site, No. 11, was drastically altered in 1966/67, when at a cost of half a million pounds, the Iveagh Trustees transformed the rear part into a seven-storey 'tower-block' of offices, with a couple of penthouses for the family above.[11] The main staircase and other features disappeared, but Adam work can still be enjoyed in ground-floor and first-floor rooms facing the Square. One of the conditions for the authorization of the tower-block was that it should not be visible from any part of the latter, and this was faithfully fulfilled.

21a. No. 4, the courtyard, the only survivor of its kind in the Square.

The main trophy surviving in No. 12 (now linked with No. 11 as the headquarters of the Advisory Conciliation and Arbitration Service – ACAS), is an exceptionally fine mid-eighteenth-century chimneypiece in the ground-floor front room.

Messrs Grindlays have a charming inheritance at No. 13, and in the entrance

22. *Three period pieces.* Right to left, *No. 5 by Matthew Brettingham snr (refronted by Cubitts, 1854); No. 6 by Fitzroy Robinson, 1962; No. 7 by Sir Edwin Lutyens, 1911.*

and banking halls at least such civilized predecessors as the Dukes of Roxburgh and the Windham Club (we shall be meeting them later) would surely appreciate the way it has been cherished. As has so often happened, the lovely staircase has also survived when so much else has been altered or clean swept away. From the leads of this corner house, by the way, one can survey a roofscape of sublime confusion, embracing not only two sides of the Square, but Ormond Yard and Mason's Yard, and Jermyn St beyond.

The northern half of the East India Club (No. 16) almost scrapes into this chapter, as being of about 1805–7 behind its Victorian façade, but nobody knows who designed it, and thanks to numerous subsequent redecorations perhaps only the chimneypiece of the first-floor drawing-room, with its charming young lady supporters (one is on p. 103), provides an authentic link with that epoch.

Nothing more on the West side (apart of course from Nos. 15 and 20, already explored), nor on the South side either, which leaves us with just the East side pair 32 and 33. Here rebuilding has taken a more than usually drastic toll. But at least a carved mitre in the big room behind the venetian windows of No. 32 reminds us that this was for over 150 years the West End mansion of the Bishops of London, while at No. 33 there has recently been a careful rehabilitation of its three or four eighteenth-century apartments.

VI

A Study in Contrasts

Dynastic Norfolk House

A character who has always delighted the devotees of St James's Square is Isabella Lady Wentworth, daughter of Sir Allan Apsley (No. 20) and mother of the 2nd Earl of Strafford of the 2nd creation (No. 5). Her letters, with their uninhibited flow of gossip and above all their dauntless spelling, spring gaily out from the massive corpus of the *Wentworth Papers*.[1] She cannot lose a pet dog without engaging our instant sympathy:

> . . . poor charming Fubs, never poor wretch had a hader death. As it leved so it dyed, full of lov leening its head in my bosom, never offered to snal at anybody in its horrid torter but nussle its head to us and lloock earnestly at me and Sue . . .

But it also happens that we have excellent passages of descriptive chatter by Lady Wentworth relating to two mansions on opposite sides of the Square, Nos. 21 and 31, which typify, in their very different ways, its architectural and social history, and seem to demand more detailed treatment than their neighbours.

No. 31 (Norfolk House) should perhaps be given precedence, not only for its long association with the Premier Dukes of England, but because (as we saw in Ch. 1) on part of the site stood the first house completed in the Square, built by Lord St Albans for his own occupation. However, by 1676 his new and much bigger mansion on the North side was already under construction and he accordingly sold out to the very active West End builder, Richard Frith. A number of brief occupancies followed, among which we need only note the fleeting presence of the Portuguese and Spanish Ambassadors (1681 and 1692) and a prophetic visitation by the 7th Duke of Norfolk (1684–85).

The Sunderlands, who came next, were heavier metal, though even they did not stay long – the 2nd Earl from 1694 to 1702, the 3rd until 1708. The former, as Secretary of State, was one of the many St James's Square adherents of William III whose ghosts, no doubt, approve his continued presence in bronze.

The 3rd Earl removed to Piccadilly, and at this point enter Lady Wentworth, househunting for her son, then Lord Raby[2] and Ambassador at the Hague:

> November 23, 1708.
>
> My dearist and best of children, I have been to see a very good hous in St. Jamsis Squair. It has thre large rooms forward and two little ons backward, closetts and marble chimney peicis, and harths to al the best rooms, and iron backs to the chimneys. Thear is twoe prety clossets with chimneys and glas over them, and picturs in the wenšcoat over most of the chimneys, bras locks to al the doars, wenscoat at bottom and top and slips of boards for the hangings. Thear will want little to be dun to it. Thear is back stairs, two coach housis, and stable for ii horses, rooms over for sarvents, very good offisis, a yard for the drying of cloaths, and leds for that purpus, a stable yard and a hors pond and back gate, which I forgot the street's name it goes into . . . To-morrow the man coms to tell me the prise . . .

Then three days later:

> My dearist and best of children, I have sent you the exact account under the gentleman's own hand; . . . thear is New Rever water in all the offisis and great led sesterns in twoe or thre playsis, the kitchin is one, and the brewhous and washhous . . . It is a noble hous and fitt for you, and strong, noe danger of its falling by great wynds; aboundenc of the new buildings fall . . .

After all this, the Sunderlands' home was rejected – as in due course was No. 21 – in favour of No. 5, town house of the Straffords from 1711 until almost our own day.

The eventual purchaser of the future Norfolk House was the 2nd Earl (later 1st Duke) of Portland, who had previously rented No. 33. And now a new and highly interesting scene opened.

With ambitious ideas about entertaining, Lord Portland decided at once that the house was inadequate as it stood, and set about erecting what can only be called a grandiose annexe at the bottom of the garden. This was the structure which, under the quite misleading name of 'Old Norfolk House', became the subject of future legend. For the time being, however, it was usually referred to as 'Lord Portland's gallery', and as such caused plentiful twittering in the Square. Plain to a fault outside, its main feature was the 'great room' at first-floor level which, as the *Survey* remarks, must have resembled in its heyday 'the *salone* of a great Venetian palazzo'.

The whole contraption, complete with wall and ceiling decorations (probably be Sebastiano Ricci), was run up with remarkable speed, and by the month of January, 1712, Portland was able to use it for what Peter Wentworth called a 'dinner, musicke and dancing' in honour of the prodigious lion of that winter season, Prince Eugene.

The Prince had come to London specifically to give support to his comrade-in-arms, John Churchill, Duke of Marlborough, then nearing disgrace. He was already too late for that, but it did not prevent huge crowds turning out to gape, and half the grandees of the Kingdom from entertaining him. St James's Square was in the thick of it – he is reported in turn at Ormonde House, at Lady Betty Germain's assembly (No. 16) and at Lady Hervey's (No. 6) – 'those two great men ye Duke of Marlborough and ye Prince Eugene honoured me both together', her husband wrote with pride.[3] The Prince's countenance, hard-featured and yellow, could certainly not match the godlike aspect of John Churchill, though we shall never know whether he deserved the ribaldry of Lady Strafford; she had taken it into her head, she told her husband, that Prince Eugene 'must have been wounded some time in the ——, for I never saw anyone sit down more stiffly'.[4]

It seems to have been a fact that (as Swift noted)[5] neither he nor Marlborough took part in the dancing at Lord Portland's famous party. Since most contemporary accounts of such affairs are in very general terms, we are fortunate in having a blow-by-blow account of this one. The document in question is among the Portland Papers held by the University of Nottingham (PWB/79), but Mr Mark Girouard's excellent summary may be quoted:

> The evening started with dinner at the late hour of six, to fit in with a sitting of the House of Lords; the normal time was now one or two o'clock. It was attended by the Prince, seventeen noblemen and no ladies. The waiting was all done by volunteer gentlemen 'that offered themselves to have an occasion to see the feast'. There was a buffet loaded with plate, and during the whole meal 'trumpets and kettle drum play'd in a room adjoining'.
>
> After dinner the company removed to Lady Portland's apartment on the first floor. Here 'several persons of both sexes had been invited to cards' and to hear a symphony performed by twenty singers and musicians from the opera. While this was going on, the saloon was cleared of tables and buffet for a ball. The company returned there at ten, and the ball lasted till three.
>
> The company then moved downstairs to Lord Portland's apartment, where supper was served. . . . Prince Eugene insisted on serving the ladies in person before he ate himself, and the other men followed his example. . . . Everyone left at about five in the morning.

Mr Girouard comments that the separation of men and women was in the medieval tradition, adding that another interesting feature was the small number of people involved – eighteen for dinner,[7] fifteen couples dancing; the affair was notable for the style and richness of the accompaniments, not because of its size.

23. Thomas Howard, 8th Duke of Norfolk. By R. Van Bleeck.

A point worth remembering when we read (as we constantly do) about 'balls' in St James's Square at that period – one should seldom if ever envisage anything on the scale of a twentieth-century 'coming out' party, or even an Oxbridge 'May Ball' or 'Commem.'.

Lord Portland stayed on until 1722, when the old house was bought for £10,000 by Trustees on behalf of the 8th Duke of Norfolk, who had already had a longish spell at No. 8. The name 'Norfolk House' was thus born in comfortable time for that meeting in March 1726 (p. 30) which would launch the 'embellishment' of St James's Square, and it has been perpetuated until now.

The 8th Duke, ever-active as a Trustee, died just before Christmas 1732, to be succeeded by his brother Edward. It seems that the house was already in some decay, but rebuilding was not contemplated yet; meanwhile, it was to be the setting for a prime St James's Square happening.

In September 1737, Frederick Prince of Wales, at odds (like all Hanoverian heirs) with his father George II, took Norfolk House furnished at a rental of £1500 per annum, and it was there that his second child, the future George III, was born (June 4 1738) – perhaps the only instance of a British monarch seeing the light of day in the house of a subject. The scene was almost certainly the main building facing the Square, *not* the Portland annexe to which future generations attached the name 'Old Norfolk House' and revered as King George's birthplace.

The royal tenants left in 1741, their departure hastened, it is said, by the rickety condition of the structure – 'cracks and failures' in the front wall. However, rebuilding, on the magnificent scale contemplated by the Duke, had to be delayed until he had acquired the site of the house next door, one of the three built by the 1st Lord Balasye. This had come into the possession of Joseph Banks MP, of Revesby Abbey, Lincolnshire. After it had been let for a time to the Prussian Minister, Count Daggenfielt, the Howards were able to acquire it in March 1748 for a mere £1830. The way was now clear for the demolition of both houses and for building operations to begin.

It is typical of St James's Square that (like Lord Portland's 'gallery') the mansion designed for the Duke by Matthew Brettingham senr was grandiose within, while presenting a face to the world which, as indicated in Chap. V, was decidedly plain pudding. Grievous though the destruction of Norfolk House in 1938 was (and inconceivable today), at least we do not have to rely totally on photographs and written descriptions of its splendours. The most lavishly decorated apartment of all, the music room, was presented happily by the 16th Duke to the Victoria & Albert Museum and (as French guide books say) *vaut bien la visite*. Though the absence of the fourth (window) wall unfortunately does give the effect of a huge alcove rather than a room, one can still savour what Desmond Fitzgerald calls in his delightful monograph its 'gilded and mirrored splendour'.[8] The best of the decoration is on the ceiling – no wonder Horace Walpole described the guests at the Duke's opening party gaping in the air 'as though there had been a comet'; in these less inhibited days we can do better by lying flat on the Museum floor to enjoy at our leisure the glorious rococo cartouches which typify Music, Painting (incorporating a full-sized easel, complete with picture of Minerva), Literature, Sculpture, Architecture (with plan of

24. *Norfolk House, the music room, with decor by Jean-Antoine Cuenot, 1755.*

24a. Norfolk House, detail of music room ceiling (representing Painting).

Norfolk House), Astronomy, Geometry and Surveying.

The whole thing is so much in the French *dix-huitième* taste that it was long deemed to have been an importation. But research at Arundel Castle has proved that the music room *boiseries* must be attributed to a certain Jean-Antoine Cuenot, an immigrant from the Franche Comté with a workshop in Warwick St, Golden Square, while the impresario for the ceiling cartouches and much of the rest of the Norfolk House decoration was Giovanni Borra, an immigrant from Piedmont.

Apart from all these sumptuosities, Mr Girouard points out[9] that the house has another claim to attention; in contrast to the usual scheme of a series of state rooms strung out along a single axis, Brettingham pioneered a central staircase leading to a circuit of apartments through which crowds of visitors could be manoeuvred, returning eventually to their starting-point. Some system of the kind was certainly necessary at that house-warming in February 1756. The crush was terrific. 'All London' was there, which meant a social setback for anyone *not* invited – usually on political grounds. Witness the 'Elegy written in an Empty Assembly Room', where Richard Cambridge dramatizes the chagrin of Lady Townshend:

> *Oh could I on my waking brain impose*
> *Or but forget at least my present woes,*
> *Forget 'em – how? each rattling coach suggests*
> *The loath'd ideas of the crowding guests . . .*
> *This night the happy and the unhappy keep*
> *Vigil alike* – Norfolk hath murdered sleep![10]

The creator of all that splendour died at Norfolk House in September 1777, aged 91 and without a son, so was succeeded by his second cousin, Charles. This 10th Duke's reign lasted only eleven years and left no great mark on the Square – in fact he lived mainly in the country where he is supposed to have 'indulged in many eccentricities'. If so, he was easily outdone by his eldest son and heir, another Charles.

A weird mixture, the 11th Duke, so familiar in Regency memoirs (Creevey's especially[11]) as 'Jockey', just as his successor was 'Little Twitch', or 'Scroop'. Since most of his family were Roman Catholics and Tories, he must needs declare himself Protestant and Whig, and a supporter of Charles James Fox on such issues as opposition to the American War. His most notorious political act was to hold a great dinner at the Crown & Anchor Tavern in the Strand, where in front of 2000 adherents he gave his own version of the loyal toast, 'Our sovereign's health – the Majesty of the People'. For this he was removed from public office, the news reaching him the very night he was entertaining the Prince Regent in St James's Square.

The Duke's personal life mingled the squalid and the splendid – he hated soap and water and his servants had to take advantage of his not infrequent drunken stupors to strip and wash him. The odd affair of the 'screaming fowls' (p. 113) somehow seems fully in character. Yet he was a great connoisseur of architecture, books and antiquities and was proud to show Creevey over Norfolk House – 'a capital magnificent shop it is', commented the diarist, whose tastes ran decidedly to gilded walls and yellow satin.

The 'Jockey' died in December 1815; once again there was no direct heir, and Bernard the 12th Duke was an even more remote cousin than the 10th. He settled quickly into the St James's Square ambiance, however, and was ready to take a lead in the comparatively hectic events of 1818 (pp. 83–6). Later in life, his attendance at Trustee meetings fell off, nor can it be said that the Square owed much to subsequent Dukes. There is in fact no trace of Norfolk House being represented at any meeting between 1860 and 1920! Nevertheless in the latter year, with Bernard, 16th Duke, still a minor,[12] his mother the Duchess was

25. Norfolk House, details of 'monkey' doorway.

26. *'A view of Norfolk' – Charles Howard, 11th Duke of Norfolk. By Dighton.*

26a. Bernard, 12th Duke of Norfolk. By Thomas Gainsborough.

invited to become a Trustee – the first official 'Lady of the Square'.

Sadly, the Duchess turned out to be yet another non-attender, and even after her son came of age he made only one appearance – in May 1935. By that time, in any case, it was widely known that the Howards were on the wing from St James's Square. Negotiations for the sale of Norfolk House had begun as early as 1928, and in July 1930 it was put on the auction block by Messrs Hampton as 'eminently suitable for a Nobleman's town house . . . or for a club, embassy or colonial office', with the significant addendum – 'An unequalled opportunity for development'. There was a tremendous rush for particulars, but when the day came, after an opening bid of £100,000 the property was withdrawn at £250,000, the auctioneer stating that much bigger offers had already been made.

Eventually the house was sold by private treaty to a company formed to exploit the site. A planning application put in for a new building by the architects Gunton & Gunton met with surprisingly slight resistance. The chief opposition came from the Georgian Group, newly formed as an offshoot of the Society for the Protection of Ancient Buildings. The London County Council itself quickly agreed to allow demolition, though the report of its Architect, on which the decision was based, makes curious reading.[13] He starts with fallacious references to 'the original Norfolk House at the rear' and 'the ceiling of the room in which George III was born', describing the former as a 'shell' and the latter as the only feature of interest – poorly preserved, but a photograph would be taken. He goes on:

> Generally speaking, there is little work of architectural merit in the house, the decorations being in the baroque style and designed by Matthew Bretenham (sic) . . . and I do not suggest that any action should be taken in regard to their preservation.

So much for eighteenth-century baroque! By then, it is true, the masterpieces of Messrs Borra and Cuenot may have become somewhat shabby and we know that the so-called 'Old Norfolk House' was a sad sight, part laundry, part a storage dump for archives. Nevertheless the music room bears witness to what was lost when in the second week in February 1938 the furnishings not removed elsewhere were sold and the demolishers could move in.

The drawing-room at Norfolk House was packed for Christie's three-day sale of pictures, furniture and silver, *The Times* commenting that the English love of a lord 'extends to his household gods'.[14] The grand total raised was £21,562, and of course the individual prices seem modest enough by modern standards – a splendid pair of mirrors £671, pair of walnut wall-lanterns by William Kent £81 18*d*, three marble mantelpieces by Brettingham £241, and so on.

Curiously enough, there was more of a struggle over the height of the successor building than over the loss of its predecessor, the developers arguing that only something exceeding the 80 ft limitation under the London Building Act of 1930 would 'add to the beauty of the Square'. Doubtful! But in any case they lost. What we now have is the 'Norfolk House' described by Sir Nikolaus Pevsner as a 'brick and stone building of no merit' – too severe no doubt, but it must be agreed that the south-east corner of the Square is today a sober scene.

However, the new Norfolk House was destined for a certain fame. A plaque on its outward wall – less legible there than on p. 136 – records how soon after its erection it was taken over as General Eisenhower's headquarters for planning the successive invasions of North Africa and Europe. The present writer has to admit that, as a minuscule member of the team there some months before D-Day, he was totally unconscious of the wartime condition of St James's Square (colour plate III).

No. 21 – From Mistresses to Bishops

Two years after her son had rejected Lord Sunderland's mansion as a London home, Lady Wentworth returned to the charge. On December 10 1710 she wrote offering him a choice of three houses, with a strong bias towards No. 21 St James's Square. As we saw in Chapter I, it had been vacated in 1696 by Katherine Sedley, Countess of Dorchester, on her marriage to Sir David Colyear, the future Earl of Portmore. A series of short lets followed, the most recent tenant being the Prussian Ambassador, Spannheim, from 1707 until his death in 1710.

Lady Wentworth had a personal interest in No. 21. It was next door to her father's old home, in fact she declares that Sir Allen Bathurst had the building of it 'at the order of King James for Lady Dorchester'. But the dear lady was in a muddle of mistresses – if Sir Allen had been involved it must have been on behalf of Arabella Churchill, Lady Dorchester's predecessor in the princely bed. However, her sales pitch was characteristic:

> The wals are of a great height, becaus none should over loock them, a prety little garden and coach hous and stables for more then oaght horsis. . . . The grownd rent is very small, not abov 15 pd. a year. Moonsear Spannyor leved thear. In the worst of thees housis one mey be very esy and happy. Neither of the other twoe have coach housis or stables belongin to them . . . Lady Dorchisters is much better, its the best in the squar . . .

Lady Wentworth says that though No. 21 cost £10,000 to build, it was now to be had for only £6000. But again no deal was struck, and it seems that the Portmores came back into residence. In 1723 in fact Lord Portmore bought the freehold from the Duchess of Buckinghamshire, his wife's daughter by King James (then Duke of York). The price this time was £6400, and he was thus able to take his place among the original St James's Square Trustees.

This first Lord Portmore died in 1730, and then his only son Charles, a genial, well-upholstered character, brought a fresh coronal of strawberry leaves into the Square by marrying the widow of Peregrine Osborne, 3rd Duke of Leeds. Eight years later he transferred No. 21 to his stepson, the future 4th Duke, who has a small but permanent niche in St James's Square mythology. It was his marriage in 1740 to Frances, daughter of Henrietta Godolphin (Duchess of Marlborough in her own right) which gave rise to the lines repeated so many years later by

Samuel Johnson, and inscribed on our title page. The verse may be hackneyed; the actual context is less well known.

Boswell had the story from their friend Bennet Langton and notes as very remarkable that Johnson 'retained in his memory trivial as well as important things'. He goes on:

> As an instance of this, it seems that an inferiour domestick [in fact a footman] of the Duke of Leeds had attempted to celebrate his Grace's marriage in such homely rhimes as he could make; and this curious composition having been sung to Dr Johnson he got it by heart, and used to repeat it in a very pleasant manner. Two of the stanzas were these—
>
> 'When the Duke of Leeds shall married be
> To a fine young lady of high quality,
> How happy will that gentlewoman be
> In his Grace of Leeds's good company.
>
> She shall have all that's fine and fair
> And the best of silk and sattin shall wear;
> And ride in a coach and take the air
> And have a house in St. James's Square.'
>
> To hear a man, of the weight and dignity of Johnson, repeating such humble attempts at poetry, had a very amusing effect. He, however, seriously observed of the last stanza repeated by him, that it nearly comprised all the advantages that wealth can give.

There was no lack of additional stanzas and alternative readings; one of the latter was a more forthright and footmanly version of the penultimate couplet:

> She shall breed young lords and ladies fair
> And ride abroad in a coach and three pair,
> And the best . . . etc.

The 4th Duke and his 'fine young lady' enjoyed an occupancy of No. 21 which was only ended by her death from apoplexy in 1764 ('went off shocking sudden', wrote a contemporary), followed by his own in 1789. The next Duke, Francis, balanced a dignified rôle in public affairs (Foreign Secretary under Pitt, 1783–91) against an unfortunate relish for low company, 'particularly players'. According to the *Farington Diary*, three bottles of claret at a sitting and gaming up to 4 a.m. were his downfall – no wonder a mortification of the bladder carried him away.

Long before that there had been a busy architectural interlude in which, as at Norfolk House, the name of Brettingham predominated. Only this time it was Matthew's grandson[16] Robert Furze who was in action. During 1790–93 he rebuilt No. 21 to what seems a sensible enough plan; the frontage, though not so extensive as that of Norfolk House, was wider than most, and Brettingham, like his grandfather, took advantage of this to provide a central entrance with staircase hall behind it and reception rooms on each side.

However, he does not seem wholly to have satisfied their Graces, because the

Duchess was soon in conclave with that favourite St James's Square house-doctor, John Soane. The latter hastened to produce what the *Survey* calls 'plans and elevations for a complete rebuilding of Brettingham's brand-new house'. Understandably, his clients balked and in the end Soane's participation was limited to minor adjustments outside and in. Altogether, the Brettingham/Soane mansion is said to have cost £38,000.

One more Duke of Leeds, George the 6th, succeeded briefly (1800–2) and then the £38,000 investment was disposed of to mortgagees for a mere £11,500. It stood empty for a while, but in 1807 the versatile club promoter George Raggett (founder of White's) loomed up and, as we shall see in Chap. XI, for the next eight years No. 21 housed his Union Club, scene of so much high play.

The club moved out in 1815. The next owner was the Earl of Bective who, early in 1818, sold the house to William Beauclerk, 8th Duke of St Albans, great-great-grandson of Charles II by Nell Gwynn – a connection typical enough of No. 21.

The 8th Duke and his son William, the 9th, were owners until 1828, though during 1821 Lord Stewart (the future 3rd Marquess of Londonderry), and his wife enjoyed a brief but flamboyant tenancy.[17] Duke William it was who, in 1827, made his celebrated marriage with the actress Harriet Mellon, widow of the millionaire banker Thomas Coutts; this obviously led the couple to migrate from St James's Square to the address in Piccadilly later identified with the Victorian philanthropies of Angela Burdett-Coutts.

* * *

If Norfolk House can be taken to represent one tendency in the Square – the establishment of a great and continuing dynasty in a mansion rebuilt for the purpose – No. 21 illustrates another – a series of richly contrasted owners or tenants replacing each other in fairly quick succession. The next turn of fortune's wheel was certainly one of the least predictable.

After the Archbishops of Canterbury and York and the Bishops of London (the last-named already dug in across the Square), the Bishops of Winchester have ranked since medieval times as the senior prelates of the English Church. Until later sub-divisions the see was vast, extending from Rotherhithe to Sark, and its revenues enormous. The Bishops' principal seat was at Farnham Castle, but the twelfth-century Bishop Giffard erected a splendid palace in Southwark, with a park of over 60 acres. In the 1640s, with South London rapidly building up, the Bishops withdrew; parts of the great house[18] were converted into factories, but it also became the nucleus of a very low quarter indeed, 'the Stews', whose fair inhabitants alas were known as 'Winchester geese'.

Subsequently a house was bought in Chelsea which the Bishops continued to occupy until 1821, when Bishop Toulmin, finding himself too far from the centre of things, obtained Parliamentary sanction to dispose of it. From the sale, a fund of £7200 was accumulated, but it was left to Toulmin's successor to turn this to account.

Charles Richard Sumner, 89th Bishop of Winchester, had reached that summit by a truly singular route. His father, the Vicar of Kenilworth, came of a vigorous Etonian/clerical family, while his mother was a Wilberforce, cousin of the famous William. At Trinity College, Cambridge, in 1810–13, young Sumner had as a fellow-undergraduate Lord Mount Charles, eldest son of the Marchioness Conyngham, George IV's last and most voluminous mistress.[19] Shortly before his ordination in 1814 he was invited by the Conynghams to act as bear-leader to Mount Charles and his younger brother Lord Francis on a continental tour.

When they reached Switzerland, however, an event took place of which markedly different accounts survive – Sumner's courtship of and eventual marriage to Jenny Fanny Barnabière Maunoir, daughter of a Geneva Professor of Surgery by his English wife. According to the future Bishop's son and biographer, Canon George Sumner,[20] Lord Conyngham had promised him either an annuity or a living if he continued to tutor his sons until both had graduated, but he asked to be released so that he could marry and settle down at once to the clerical life. Conyngham agreed, and Sumner was duly installed as curate at Highclere in Hampshire (1816). However, four years later his younger pupil, Lord Francis, was made Master of the Robes and First Groom of the Bedchamber to King George IV, and the Highclere curate was quickly summoned to dinner at Brighton Pavilion.

Thus Canon Sumner, who with one passing exception, makes no reference whatever to the existence of the *Marchioness* Conyngham.

For a more sensational version of the Sumner/Conyngham connection, we can turn to the normally sober pages of the *Dictionary of National Biography*. There the belief is recorded that the newly ordained parson married the surgeon's daughter to prevent Lord Mount Charles from doing so, and that the boy's father put him on the road to fortune out of gratitude.[21]

What is beyond doubt is that, once arrived at Court, Charles Sumner made a stunning hit with the King. That very first evening they are said to have conversed for over three hours, His Majesty lying on a sofa while his guest stood behind it. 'Your fortune is made,' said Lord Francis, and almost instantly came an offer from the King of a Canonry at Windsor. The Prime Minister, Lord Liverpool, and the entire Cabinet reared up, and after paroxysms of royal outrage and despair, the King transferred the Canonry to Dr James Clarke, thus leaving vacant for Sumner the appointments of Private Chaplain, Librarian and Historiographer Royal, with 'a capital house opposite the Park Gates' at Windsor.

Here was something to set all Brighton and St James's a-buzz. Writing to Metternich (January 8 1822), the redoubtable Russian Ambassadress, Princess Lieven, enjoyed the situation no end, though (like Lady Wentworth with the mistresses) she got her denominations a bit mixed up:

> I believe I neglected to tell you of a new character who has entered the lists at Brighton . . . He is a Methodist parson, a young man of 28, handsome and healthy; he enjoys the confidence of the favourite, he is her spiritual director, and he

27. Bishop Charles Sumner, who made No. 21 into 'Winchester House'.

> exercises spiritual and temporal control over all the King's movements . . . He sits opposite the King, and prays aloud before dinner. They listen to him very piously, which looks extremely comic.[22]

The 'Methodist parson' whose influence over the King was undoubtedly for the good, was not destined merely for a courtier's career. One preferment after another was showered upon him, culminating in the simultaneous Bishopric of Llandaff and Deanery of St Paul's (March 1826), followed only a year later by the offer of Winchester, made it seems by the King entirely of his own volition.

Thus at the age of thirty-eight Charles Sumner was raised to what his contemporaries saw as 'the pinnacle of worldly prosperity, wealth and all that is incidental to high station'. It must be added at once that, by whatever road he got there, Sumner proved to be a prelate of prime nineteenth-century vintage, intelligent, charming and incredibly industrious.

One of the first matters to be settled was that of a town house. He quickly fixed on No. 21. Writing in 1876, when already there was 'every probability that this house would pass away from the See', Canon Sumner tells the story in some detail. Against £21,500 demanded by the Duke of St Albans, only £7200 was available from the Chelsea transaction. The Bishop, practical as ever, consulted his 'woodward' at Farnham, who assured him that there were vast quantities of timber which ought to be felled. Even this required an Act of Parliament (quickly obtained with the blessing of the Archbishop of Canterbury and the Lord Chancellor) and some £14,500 worth of episcopal timber completed the purchase price.

It might be asked why the Bishop of a gigantic diocese in Southern England, with several subsidiary residences as well as Farnham Castle, needed a house in St James's Square at all. There are two answers to this. One is that in addition to his ecclesiastical duties, the Bishop of Winchester was a political figure, an active member of the House of Lords, up to his eyes in Catholic Emancipation and the Reform Bill, as well as his ceremonial rôle as Prelate to the Order of the Garter; the other, that he also had the almost terrifying commitment of evangelizing the densely populated jungle of South London which now forms the Diocese of Southwark. Sumner's practice was to spend spring and early summer – the London 'season' in fact – at No. 21, where meetings of and hospitality to the hard-pressed clergy of Lambeth or Bermondsey alternated with more fashionable soirées, through which the Bishop moved, dignified and kind.

This remarkable episcopate, in the course of which Sumner claimed to have consecrated some 300 new or rebuilt churches and enlarged 200 others, lasted no less than forty-one years. In 1869 he took advantage of a timely act of Parliament allowing Bishops to retire, and was succeeded by Bishop Wilberforce ('Soapy Sam'). But Sumner's happiness over this was turned into mourning when his second cousin and protegé lived only three years more, his death preceding his own by thirteen months. The next incumbent, Dr Browne, occupied the house even more briefly before it was sold, so the history of No. 21 as 'Winchester House' is to all intents and purposes that of the life work of Charles Sumner.

* * *

The reason why Bishop Browne remained such a short time in St James's Square was that the Ecclesiastical Commissioners needed money for a specific purpose, the endowment of the new Bishopric of St Albans – and what more appropriate source! The inevitable Act of Parliament went through, and after No. 21 had been offered unsuccessfully by auction in 1875 and 1876, the Commissioners accepted a

28. No. 20 as Messrs. Hampton's offices, with empty site of No. 21 alongside (about 1935).

bid of £45,000 from the Treasury. There had been some idea that the house might be taken over by the Army & Navy Club, and the *Survey* notes the Bishop's warning that in that case 'provision should be made for removing the window glass full of the sacred monogram I H S'.

In the event, No. 21 became a branch of the War Office, and as such in 1881 was to attract the Fenian menace to that corner of the Square. Other Government departments followed on until 1924, when the Centaur Club[23] took over. From 1927 No. 21 was on the market again, and then in 1933 Commander E. W. B. Leake came forward with an ambitious scheme to demolish the house and build an elaborate headquarters for the National Sporting Club. The promoters got so far as pulling down the old house in order to clear the site, but for various reasons the whole project fell through. The *Survey* quotes a remark in *The Architect and Building News* (which published a drawing of the proposed clubhouse), regretting the destruction of the 'dignified and admirable façade' of No. 21, adding:

> What passes comprehension is that it should be possible for a square as famous and distinguished as St James's to be rebuilt in the way it is, without regard to unity or continuity.

A just and oft-repeated stricture, though it happens that it could hardly be applied to the eventual fate of No. 21. Next door to it stood Robert Adam's even more distinguished No. 20. When the Strathmores moved out in 1921 (p. 137), it became the West End headquarters of Messrs Hampton, who made their presence known in a way which might be frowned upon today (p. 71). Then in 1935, the Distillers' Company acquired both No. 20 and the vacant site of No. 21. They carefully restored the former and commissioned the architectural partnership of Mewès & Davis to put an office block on the latter, but with a façade identical with No. 20's. This was carried out with almost miraculous fidelity, and though purists may argue that it would not have been Robert Adam's solution, it remains a monument of 1930s craftsmanship.

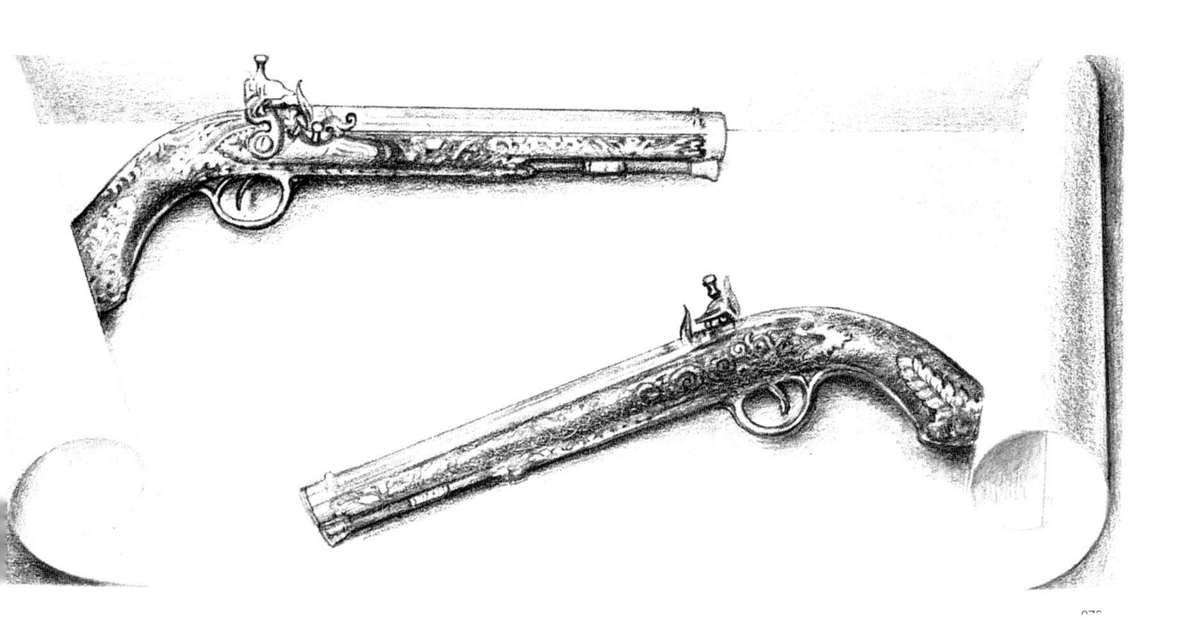

VII
Disturbers of the Peace

Anyone who might assume that life in St James's Square, as governed by the Act of 1726, proceeded with the decorous rhythm of a minuet, must be unacquainted with the works of William Hogarth. As far as one recalls, the Square itself does not happen to figure in them, but they do convey, with piercing force, the interplay of rough and smooth, of brutalism and civility, which was the pattern of eighteenth-century West End life, continued into Regency times and – Bishops notwithstanding – was never quite smothered under the blanket of Victorian decorum. We can now explore something of this darker side.

From the start, the Trustees were much preoccupied with law and order. Some alarming past events in the Square must have still been present in their minds when they commenced their duties. They might have recalled, for example, the anti-papal riots of 1688. With King James II already on the wing, a rabble appeared before No. 8, then tenanted by M. Barillon, the French Ambassador. Fortunately Barillon, along with several neighbours, had applied for military protection, and the would-be looters, confronted by a considerable body of troops, carried their destructive intentions elsewhere. Or, on a different plane, the night in November 1692, when '13 rogues' broke into Ormonde House and the room where the Duke's plate and jewellery were kept, before being apprehended. Vandalism too was not absent – witness the reward of 2 gns offered for the detection of the thief who in August 1705 'mischievously cut down and carried away' one of the trees in front of Lord Radnor's house (No. 7).

Though the Trustees decided, at a very early meeting (May 1727), to appoint two 'sober persons' as night watchmen, at £13 per annum, it may be doubted – again on the evidence of Hogarth (to say nothing of William Shakespeare) – whether they were very dynamic guardians of the peace; better perhaps at 'calling the hours' between 10 pm and 6 am, and snoozing meanwhile in their 'portable watch houses' than in coping with malefactors. One can hardly, for example, envisage them intervening very effectively in the desperate mugging of Mr Rambouillet, 'Lieutenant of Grenadiers and Quarter-Master of the first Regiment of Guards', as reported during the August of their first year's service. Lieutenant Rambouillet, it appears, was

> set upon by five foot robbers in York Street, near St James's Square, three of them keeping their pistols presented at his body, while the others rifled him of a diamond ring, a broad piece, two guineas and a half and a silver watch, together with his hat, periwig and cane.[1]

The villains told him to kneel down while they made their escape, but one of them turned back suddenly and 'cut him about the head in a barbarous manner', and they all got safely away.

Highwaymen continued to be a menace, even in the heart of London, until much later. Horace Walpole records how in February 1773 two daughters of Admiral Holborn were stopped 'as their carriage was conveying them across St James's Square' – a safe enough transit one would have thought – and they had to give up their watches, jewels and rings.[2] A year later Lady Mary Coke, commenting that 'the street robbing which had subsided' was starting up again, instances two other ladies being set upon in the little street (John St) adjoining Norfolk House.[3] It seems that in both cases, as usual, the assailants escaped unscathed. Watchmen, what of the night!

They may have done rather better in chasing off vagrants, who indeed can be a nuisance in the Square to this day, climbing over the railings to sleep in the bushes and leaving their rubbish around. The watchmen also seem to have been brave enough to tackle a gentleman for 'improper behaviour' (unspecified) in the Square, putting the Trustees to some expense in consequence (Minute of April 1794). One cannot help speculating what they made of the two poorly dressed young men, lacking a lodging but brimful of patriotism, who walked round and round the Square for several hours one night in 1737, 'inveighing against the Minister and resolving to stand by their country'. The two were of course Samuel Johnson and his slightly off-beat friend, Richard Savage. Curiously, the real point of that celebrated anecdote has been ignored – the 'minister' was Sir Robert Walpole, then or very recently in residence at No. 32, so this looks like a deliberate sortie into enemy country.

Reverting to 'highway robbery', this was again the charge in the notorious Driscoll case, though in fact it was a matter of extortion with menaces. The story has a painfully modern ring. Matthias John Driscoll was a well-known neighbourhood 'baddy', who in 1819 needed cash to pay a doctor to cure him of the

29. Samuel Johnson. By Sir Joshua Reynolds.

pox. His chosen method was homosexual blackmail of one of the Duke of Norfolk's footmen, Thomas Wood. In spite of walking round and round the Square (like Johnson and Savage!), so as not to reveal where he worked, Wood could not escape his tormentor. However, the landlord of the pub just outside the Norfolk House back entrance in Charles II St gave the rather dim-witted young man some sensible advice – 'go to His Grace'. Wood did so; the Duke (Bernard the 12th) satisfied himself that there was not the slightest foundation for Driscoll's allegations against him; and launched a private prosecution at his own expense. The trial did not come on until April 1821, but in July of that year, Driscoll was hanged.[4]

* * *

Yet another class of disturbers of the peace – the duellists – were not lacking among the residents. Lord Purbeck,[5] the first occupant of No. 16 (1676–78), is said to have fought there, but in general the Square itself, even in its roughest days, was considered too public a place for such encounters. But one duel at least had fierce repercussions in St James's and beyond. It also gained a fictional immortality.

For a short period in 1710–12, No. 32 was let to James, 4th Duke of Hamilton. Proud, ambitious and of royal descent, he was long suspected of designs on the Scottish and even the United Kingdom throne for himself. Nevertheless he was active in the Jacobite cause; he had advised Mary of Modena to attempt a Scottish rising at the time of the Act of Settlement (1701); now he was urging James, the Old Pretender, to come to Scotland and remain there until Queen Anne's expected death. He was therefore the obvious choice of the Tory leaders, Oxford and Bolingbroke, to go to Paris as Ambassador, briefed to reconcile James and Anne and thus to secure the Jacobite succession.

This was in November 1712. But on the eve of his departure all London – and Paris too – was stunned to hear that the great Duke had perished in a duel with Lord Mohun in Hyde Park.

The background to this affair was a dispute over the Gawsworth estate, to which both the Duchess and Lady Mohun laid claim, though there were many to suspect that the Duke had been 'set up' by the Whigs. Charles, 5th Lord Mohun, a sinister character enough, had twice been charged with murder before he was 20, and now he was in his element. The duel took place in the early hours of November 15, and was a desperate business. The parties fought three a side; the principals' swords struck home simultaneously; Mohun fell dead and Hamilton is alleged to have been stabbed on the ground by his opponent's villainous second, Major-General Macartney. He was carried back dying to St James's Square, where his Duchess was still asleep.

One of the first to hear the news was Dr Jonathan Swift. He sent round at once to the Square where (his man reported) there was 'a great rabble about the house' and the porter could not speak for tears.[6] Swift himself followed up in melancholic mood, though on a visit to the Duchess two months later he 'raged, stormed and railed'.

For ardent Jacobites it was just one more blow to their oft-delayed hopes. But it also shattered the ambitions of Miss Beatrix Esmond to whom, by one of his most audacious strokes, Thackeray betrothes the Duke – her trousseau all ready for their wedding on the eve of His Grace's departure to France.[7]

Hamilton's real-life widow stayed on three years longer at No. 32, and then the house lay empty and dark for a while.

* * *

Civil disorders – and there was no lack of them – were well beyond the competence of the poor old watchmen, or 'beadles' as they came to be called. The yell of 'Wilkes and Liberty!' must have caused many an aristocratic heart to miss a beat as supporters of the great demagogue raged round the West End as well as the City in April 1768, chalking '45' on fashionable front doors and coaches. '45' was notorious enough as the issue of the *North Briton* where Wilkes had hurled defiance at the government, and which in consequence was condemned to be burnt by the common hangman. But it must have strangely confused the Austrian Ambassador, Count Seilern, returning one night to his residence, No. 9, to be dragged from his coach and have the mystic figure applied to the soles of his shoes.

Wilkes himself, as it happens, was to lose some of his popularity with the mob when, as Lord Mayor of London, he took a hand in suppressing the 1780 riots identified with the name of Lord George Gordon. Here was a revival of that anti-papal venom which put No. 8 in such peril in the days of M. Barillon. This time, however, the epicentre was the most venerable of London Squares – Bloomsbury – where Lord Mansfield's mansion was pitilessly sacked and then burnt, and the ex-Lord Chief Justice was lucky to escape with his life.[8] St James's Square endured a lot of noise but no destruction. We should, however, note one very odd story, recorded by Papworth;[9] according to this, when King William's statue was set up in 1808, the 'persons employed in this labour' had to drain the basin, and there, among other curiosities, they found the keys of Old Newgate Gaol, apparently jettisoned by the Gordon rioters, some twenty years before. The present whereabouts of these relics, if preserved, is unknown.

Later still, the fact that the unpopular Lord Castlereagh occupied No. 18 made it something of a magnet for disorder. For example, protests over the Corn Law Bill of 1816 led to a riot of which Capt. Gronow has left us a spirited account. He says that he was walking to the Square from St James's Palace, where he had been on guard, when he beheld collected together thousands (?) of the lowest of the London rabble. These ruffians, he says,

> with loud shouts and threats of summary justice against the Ministry, were at the time I arrived breaking the windows of most of the houses in the Square. The Life Guards were patrolling the adjacent streets and whenever they appeared were received with volleys of stones mingled with mud and cries of 'Down the Piccadilly butchers!'.
>
> The mob were evidently bent on mischief and I beheld one man exciting the crowd to force the doors of the Bishop of London's residence [No. 32]. As the fellow was making a rush against it I told him to desist or I would immediately run my sword through him. This threat had the effect of calming this gentleman's ardour and he skulked away . . .[10]

30. Queen Caroline leaving No. 17 for the House of Lords, 1820.

In King St, Gronow continues, he was accosted by Lord Castlereagh himself, calmly looking on in his blue coat buttoned up to the chin, blue spencer, long gaiters, shoes covered with galoshes, and a white neck-cloth. 'The mob is not so dangerous as you think,' remarked his lordship.

William Rush, the American Envoy,[11] also noted, when he visited Lord Castlereagh in 1819, that the mansion had 'lately suffered much, especially in the windows' from the violence of the mob in a late Westminster Election, though it is not clear whether he was referring to the same disturbance recorded by Gronow.

For sheer nuisance value, however, none of these scenes can have rivalled those which disrupted the life of the Square for several weeks on end in the summer of 1820. The focus was again on the West side, but at No. 17 this time, next door to Lord Castlereagh and long the home of Sir Philip Francis. He died in 1818, but two years later his widow let the house to Queen Caroline, whose celebrated 'trial' for adultery before the House of Lords was just coming on.

Though Caroline then lived at Brandenburgh House, Hammersmith, she reckoned it an excellent propaganda ploy to rent No. 17 and drive daily down to Westminster. Immense crowds of her supporters assembled to bawl their heads off when the 'injured Queen' appeared – some of them in fact (putting their purses where their hearts were) rented places at 1*s* a time on wagons driven into the

Square in the early hours to act as grandstands. No wonder Lord Castlereagh, sadly aware of his vulnerability, closed his shutters and sent his valuables down to the country. It was not until November 1820 that the Bill of Pains and Penalties against the Queen was withdrawn, but long before that she had exhausted the publicity value of 17 St James's Square.

Watchmen continued to be appointed well into the nineteenth century, with no increase of efficiency. In April 1804 (sinking their proud independence for once) the Trustees asked the Watch Committee of St James's Parish to arrange for the 'parish patrols' to include the Square in their rounds and to report any neglect by the watchmen. Twelve years later, Samuel Thornton, the pious banker at 'No. 21a', complained of the disorderly behaviour of street-walkers in the Square, and suggested that the parish officers should be asked to 'co-operate with the beadles'. Finally, it was decided to supplement the latter with 'Square patrols', and this system continued until the epoch-making Police Act of 1830 rendered such makeshift arrangements obsolete. It could not, however, guarantee the Square against villainy or violence. We have Fenians and Libyans still to come!

VIII
From Gravell'd Walk to Garden

In Chap. IV we quoted what James ('Athenian') Stuart – if indeed he was the author of *Critical Observations on the Buildings and Improvements of London* – had to say about the design of what he called 'street houses'. But he could be equally pungent when it came to matters of town-planning.

After a dig or two at the City Fathers for what they had been up to east of Temple Bar,[1] he suggests that 'our pretensions to superiority in the west end of the town are based more on presumption than on truth'. As a test case, he launches at once into a critique of 'our so-much-vaunted squares'. His own recipe for the perfect square or public *place* is unequivocal. It should be:

> a large opening, free and unencumbered, where not only carriages have room to turn and pass but even where the people are able to assemble occasionally without confusion . . . The side or circumference should be built in a stile above the common; and churches and public edifices ought to be properly introduced. In the middle there ought to be some fountain, group or statue, railed to within a small compass; or perhaps only a bason of water which, if not so ornamental, still, by its utility in cases of fire etc., makes ample amends.

To illustrate his theme, he brings forward St JAMES's SQUARE. 'Though far from perfect in that style,' he admits, 'and altogether uncompleted on one side, it still strikes the mind (I judge from my own feeling) with something of more ease and propriety than any square in London. You are not confined in your space; your eye takes in the whole compass at a glance, and the water in the middle seems placed there for ornament and use.'

31. James 'Athenian' Stuart, architect of No. 15 and critic of London squares. Engraving by W. C. Edwards from the painting by Proven.

What a contrast, he continues, with almost every other London square, all formed on quite a different plan; to his eye they are gardens, they are sheep-walks – in other words, everything but what they should be. The *rus in urbe* is a preposterous idea at best; a garden in a street is not less absurd than a street in a garden; he that wishes to have a row of trees before his door in town 'betrays almost as false a taste as he who would build a row of houses as an avenue to his seat in the country'.

After that broadside, the author 'descends to particulars', beginning with Grosvenor Square, 'generally held out as a pattern of perfection of its kind'. Spacious, regular and well built, no doubt, but how was this spaciousness occupied? 'A clumsy rail, with lumps of brick for piers . . . encloses nearly the whole area, intercepting almost entirely the view of the sides, and leaving the passage round it as narrow as most streets . . . the middle filled up with bushes and dwarf trees, through which a statue peeps, like a piece of gilt gingerbread in a greengrocer's stall.'

The author enjoys himself even more at the expense of Cavendish Square. Here, he says, the apparent intention was to excite pastoral ideas in the mind by cooping up a few frightened sheep within a wooden paling, which if it were not for their sooty fleeces and meagre carcasses, would be more apt to give the idea of a butcher's pen. 'To see the poor things starting at every coach and hurrying round their narrow bounds requires a warm imagination to convert the scene into . . . ideas of innocence and a pastoral life.'

Hanover Square he hardly knows what to make of – 'every convenience is railed out and every nuisance railed in' – though he admits that St George's Church portico, seen in profile, enriches and beautifies the whole.

As for Red Lion Square, 'elegantly so-called no doubt from some alehouse formerly at the corner', it does not make him laugh, it makes him cry. The rough sod, the four watch houses at the corners, like so many family vaults, the naked obelisks which spring from the rough grass like a disconsolate widow's monument to her first husband – it is all a *memento mori* more powerful than a death's head and crossed marrow-bones; 'it only needs the parish bull bellowing at the gate to compleat the impression of a country churchyard'.

All the other squares, seemingly, were tinctured with the same absurdity – 'an awkward imitation of the country, amid the smoke and bustle of the town'.

* * *

By now it will have crossed any alert reader's mind that the theory of the picturesque being attacked by 'Athenian' Stuart in 1774 was the very one destined to sweep away the features of our Square which, in his eyes, set it above all others. The process, however, burnt with a very slow fuse. It was not until a meeting on May 14 1799 that the first suggestion for a change in the central area was brought forward, and all that was then agreed was that the enclosure should be altered from an octagon to a circle and that a 'respectable tradesman' should be employed to do it. Nothing more about this biggish job in the Minutes, but the Ackermann view of 1812 would seem to confirm that it did come to pass.

A further eighteen years went by before the spirit of innovation stirred again, and then it was not in the main body of Trustees but among the members of a

32. The Square in 1812. By R. Ackermann.

special 'Committee for Lighting the Square' which had been set up late in 1816. To get the lighting question out of the way first, we may note that the Committee eventually agreed (January 1818) that the Clerk should enquire from the Gas Light Company on what terms it would light 'about six lamps' round the enclosure, and at what intervals they ought to be placed. In the end, some twelve lamps were either converted to gas or newly installed, with an additional one on the South side when the inhabitants there agreed to erect four or more in front of their houses at their own expense. They would also be allowed to protect their lamps with a kerb – again provided they paid for it themselves! This they seemingly did, but at the March 1819 meeting the Trustees conceded that the lighting of the 'private lamps' should be paid for out of the General Fund.

The whole story represents uncharacteristically bold pioneering by the St James's Square Trust. Experiments in street lighting by coal gas had been demonstrated during 1808–10 in Pall Mall, but the legend that the latter was the first London thoroughfare to be regularly lit in this way has been disproved: it was St James's Square which took the lead, followed by Piccadilly and one or two adjoining areas, with Pall Mall coming third in 1820.[2]

Meanwhile a whole series of proposals for 'enlarging the present enclosure' had been brought before the Lighting Committee and for a time impeded its negotiations with the gasmen. Lord Hardwicke produced one on June 18 1817, and on the 21st the Duke of Norfolk came forward with three – not bad for an obscure country cousin who had only succeeded to the title two years before! One of his schemes (reckoned to cost about £800 against Lord Hardwicke's £625) was actually accepted. We know nothing of the details, but they do not greatly matter since even His Grace's ideas were swept aside when a portentous new figure suddenly came in view. This was 'Mr Nash' – in other words, John Nash, favourite architect of the Prince Regent and the most innovatory town planner London has ever had.

What, one wonders, can have diverted his energies into the small backwater of St James's Square, just when he was in full flight as the designer of the 'New Street' (Regent St) and the magnificent development of Portland Place, Regent's Park and so much else in the public domain? Nash's surviving papers and plans shed no light at all; one can only guess that though few if any members of the Regent's intimate circle lived in the Square, its social prestige and the presence of so many Dukes and other potential clients was sufficient bait. Yet it was one of the Square's rare commoners, Samuel Thornton of '21a', who at a full meeting of Trustees on October 17 1817 submitted a plan 'presented by Mr Nash' for laying out and planting, accompanied by an offer by that gentleman to 'superintend the execution gratuitously'. The Trustees hastened to agree and in due course Nash announced that if the Square could be 'cleared' by the second week in January, that would be the earliest that he could attend to the work.

The Trustees had already decided, in their usual thrifty fashion, that they would pay for the scheme if possible by the sale of old paving stones. Their first approach, naturally enough, was to the 'Commissioners of the New Street', but in the end it was a certain Mr Goudge of Spital Street who made an acceptable bid of £600, though even he had to be warned that unless he got on with the job 'by Saturday', the Trustees would 'resort to their Act of Parliament' to coerce him. A unique (and, one would think, fairly shaky) threat of 1726 sanctions, but it seems to have worked.

The John Nash scenario continued to expand, as a somewhat muddled Minute of May 18 1818 reveals:

> The Plan for laying out the Square being taken into consideration and it appearing that the expence of enclosing the Basin with a proper and sufficient Iron Fence would be equal to the expence of filling it up – and that if continued (as it would no longer be used for the purpose of watering the Square) it would be desireable to adopt some means of frequently changing the water.

This is the first we have heard of the fence, or of abolishing the basin either, though there had obviously been mutterings. A letter now addressed to each inhabitant went still further; at a meeting to be held at Norfolk House on Saturday morning following they would be asked to vote on whether

> The statue should be moved to the North side of the Square or to some other convenient site, and the present site occupied by a *jet d'eau*, *or*
> The basin should be filled up and the area now covered with water be planted, *or*
> The basin should stay as it was.

33. John Nash, called in to re-design the gardens in 1827. By J. A. Courigher.

Came Saturday morning, and the question of retaining the basin having been resolved in the affirmative, Mr Nash agreed to provide an estimate for moving the statue and substituting the *jet d'eau*. The former, it turned out, could be done for only £50, but a main to supply the latter would cost £250, plus £50 per annum for water (including 20 gns already payable), plus the expense of the fountain itself, dependent on design. So the statue stayed put; trenching of the ground for the proposed belt of planting within the enlarged enclosure could go ahead (Lord Hardwicke and Mr Byng to keep an eye, along with any other Trustees who might be around); and Mr Nash would set out the ground inside the belt with a view to planting in the autumn.

However, when the Trustees reconvene on June 6, a completely fresh set of characters confront us – the ladies of the Square, never heard from before and only once since (formally at any rate). They were invited to meet the Trustees at Norfolk House, Mr Nash to attend with the plans.

Six turned up – the Duchess of St Albans (No. 21), the Countess of Surrey (No. 31),[3] Viscountess Falmouth (No. 2), Lady Grantham (No. 1), and Mrs Boehm (No. 16). Lady Surrey, Lady Grantham and Mrs Boehm brought along their husbands.

In the event, the ladies' main interest turned out to be in the erection of an inner railing round the basin, no doubt for the safety of children or grandchildren playing in the garden, and an iron fence 'leaning outward from the water' was actually agreed upon. No illustration of this contrivance (which can hardly have added elegance to the scene) has come down to us, and indeed we have only a somewhat sketchy impression of Nash's layout as a whole. What we do know is that he enlarged the enclosure to its present size and shape, and that it had a belt of shrubs round the perimeter and a pattern of serpentine paths in Nash's Regent's Park manner – the pattern in fact which, though elaborated after the basin was at last filled in, was not superseded until the eve of World War I. Whether the ladies met again is not clear, though they were supposed to see Mr Nash's final scheme.

The nurseryman chosen to carry out the planting was Mr Lee, but no one will be surprised that his bill (£199 17*s* 9*d* – on the good old 'eleven three farthings' principle) 'exceeded the expectations of the Trustees' and Mr Nash was asked to vet it. Nor did London's busiest architect at that epoch disdain to plot the ground in person ('payment to Frost for stakes for Mr Nash in laying out the Square, £4 14*s* 6*d*') and it was he again who produced plans and an estimate (£100) for a Garden Seat to be presented by the Duke of Northumberland – the very summerhouse which graces the south side of the garden to this day (p. 80).

The iron railing round the basin cost £130 (Messrs May & Morritt) and the general work on enlargement carried out by a Mr Warton brought the total charges to about £700, in addition presumably to what the Trustees made by flogging their old paving stones. It was agreed that the best way of meeting the bill would be to ask the inhabitants to put up an extra year's rate rather than to borrow the money at interest, against future income.

* * *

So for the time being the basin survived. The supplying of it, together with the watering of the Square, was now entrusted to the Grand Junction Water Company, though only after a stiff tussle over terms which added considerably to the rush of meetings in June–July 1818 – perhaps the busiest period in the whole history of the Trust.

It is difficult for us today to imagine what the Square looked like with this substantial lake at the centre of its enclosure. William Weir, writing in 1843, has the interesting point that the 'circular sheet of water . . . makes little appearance from the *pavé*, but is a beautiful ornament as seen from the first-floor windows' (those of virtually all the Square drawing-rooms, of course).[4] Certainly, to keep it clean was a perennial problem, and as late as 1849 a carpenter named Fitch was

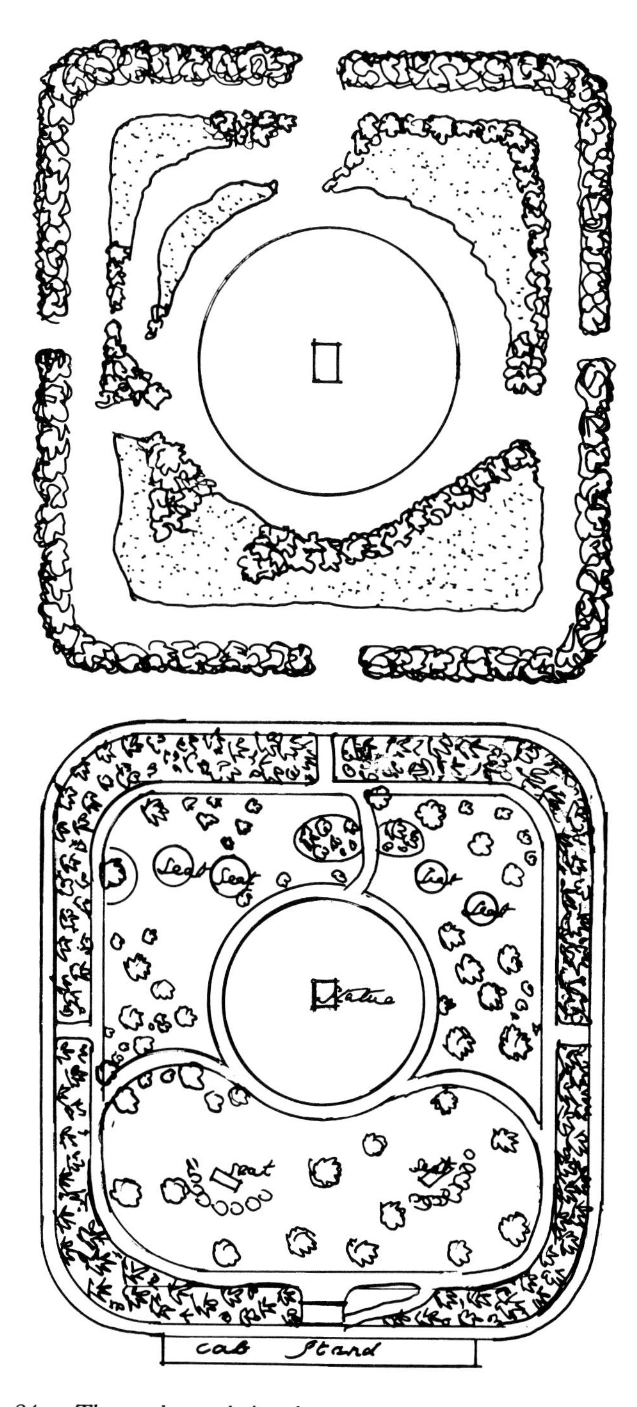

34. *The garden re-designed:*
(a) John Nash's layout incorporating the basin, 1818.
(b) The layout after filling in the basin, 1854.

paid £4 12*s* 6*d* for constructing a *punt* to be used on this job. This, incidentally, is the only recorded instance of navigation on the basin, if one excepts the lady being apparently poled along in a gondola (page 32). But she may be a flight of the artist's fancy. The removal of 'scum' and the inflow of fresh water went on until the spring of 1854 and then suddenly, and almost silently, the basin itself vanished.

It happens that around that time minute-taking was more than usually scrappy, no doubt because of the illness and subsequent death of the Clerk, Mr Roberts. All that is mentioned on the subject at the 1854 meeting (May 20) is that 'some of the Trustees having suggested some alterations in the garden and pond in the Square, my Lord de Grey (Chairman) ordered a survey and plans to be prepared'. An additional rate of 1*s* would cover the charge for 'grubbing up some of the objectionable trees, thinning the shrubs and cleaning the pond once or twice a year'.

How surprising therefore to find 'Additional Minutes' appended which refer, head-on, to 'estimates for the probable cost of filling up the pond' and to an extra 3*s* rate being sufficient to 'meet the emergency'. The writer goes on to say that too few Trustees having been present on the 20th, Lord de Grey wrote round asking for written support for this proposal. Considering that he had got it, he proceeded 'with their presumed sanction' to order the lowest tenderer, Mr McArthur, to carry out the work at a cost of £210. All of which clearly shocked the next Clerk, Mr Lee.

Dasent links this very abrupt decision to abolish the basin with the cholera scares of the mid-century, and no doubt the trees, overhanging by this time, produced a fairly slimy and sinister effect. But Lord de Grey was one of those forceful chairmen whose services the Trust periodically enjoys, and it is quite likely that, bored with the whole business of the basin and its scum, he announced one morning at breakfast, 'I'm going to have the damned thing filled up!'

IX

Interlude – The 'Other' No. 10

In his final, retrospective chapter, Dasent remarks that if the names of former inhabitants of St James's Square were to be systematically recorded, the walls of nearly every house would be 'tessellated with medallions and riddled with inscriptions'. Among those commemorated would certainly be holders of all the great offices of State, including – according to Dasent – no fewer than fifteen Prime Ministers. Here is his roll-call:

Arthur Capel, 1st Earl of Essex (No. 19, resident 1677–83)
Laurence Hyde, 1st Earl of Rochester (No. 13, 1676–77)
John Belasyse, 1st Baron (No. 32, 1688–89)
Charles Talbot, 1st Duke of Shrewsbury (No. 3, 1695; No. 5, 1696)
Charles Montagu, 1st Earl of Halifax (No. 21, 1697–1700)
Charles Howard, 3rd Earl of Carlisle (No. 3, 1696–97)
Sir Robert Walpole (later 1st Earl of Orford) (No. 32, 1732–35)
Charles Spencer, 3rd Earl of Sunderland (No. 31, 1703–08)
Spencer Compton, 1st Earl of Wilmington ('No. 21a', 1720–43)
William Pitt (later 1st Earl of Chatham) (No. 10, 1759–62)
George Grenville, 1st Baron (No. 20, 1789–92)
Robert Jenkinson, 1st Earl of Liverpool (No. 6, 1803–06)
Charles Grey, 2nd Earl Grey (No. 15, 1819)
Edward Stanley, 14th Earl of Derby (No. 10, 1837–54, No. 33, 1854–69)
William Ewart Gladstone (No. 10, 1890)

35–37. Three Prime Ministers associated with No. 10: William Pitt, 1st Earl of Chatham (W. Hoare); Edward Stanley, 14th Earl of Derby (F. R. Say); William Ewart Gladstone (J. E. Millais).

The earlier part of this list reminds one irresistibly of Lord Derby's 'Who? Who?' Cabinet of 1852, so christened from the deaf Duke of Wellington's exclamations as the unfamiliar names were read out. Doctrine today is that the office of Prime Minister only became acknowledged as such during the long reign of Sir Robert Walpole (1715–17, 1721–42). There were plenty of dominant Ministers before him, of course, from Cardinal Wolsey onwards, but none of them figures in Dasent's list. What Essex, Rochester, Belasyse, Shrewsbury, Halifax and Carlisle had in common was that each, for brief periods in the seventeenth or early eighteenth century, held what had always been regarded as the senior Cabinet post of First Lord of the Treasury. Even Sunderland, all-powerful as Secretary of State between Walpole's two terms, was never recognized as Prime Minister.

It is a little sad that perhaps the dimmest holder of the great office, Lord Wilmington (figurehead Prime Minister 1742–43, when George II was desperately seeking an alternative to Walpole), had one of the longest periods of residence in the Square, whereas Grenville (P.M. 1806–07), Liverpool (P.M. 1812–27) and Grey (P.M. 1830–34) were no more than birds of passage.

We are left with another and more majestic trio – William Pitt the elder, Derby and Gladstone. Thanks to them, No. 10 St James's Square is unique in two senses – it is almost certainly the only house in London (the senior No. 10 excepted!) to have sheltered three Prime Ministers, and the only one in the Square to have achieved one of Dasent's 'medallions'.[1]

British television viewers in the autumn of 1985 will have been made aware that No. 10 Downing Street was created as a Prime Ministerial residence by Walpole in 1735, yet No. 10 St James's Square can claim the further distinction that in spite of this, two of its three Premiers continued to live there while in office. In the case of William Pitt (not yet Earl of Chatham) this was no doubt because he was never First Lord of the Treasury, the Minister to whom No. 10 Downing St is still theoretically assigned; in terms of protocol he was merely Secretary of State throughout his St James's Square period, which included the glorious 'Year of Victories' (1758).

Although Pitt tended to divide his time between his Town house and his beloved Kentish home at Hayes, his household bills for the former, in a typical year, came to what Carrington[2] calls the 'very large sum of money for those days' of £2758, including extra stabling for his saddle horses. The butcher's bill alone amounted to £248. There was a horde of servants and hangers-on to feed no doubt, but the pressure of business also demanded the services of various secretaries or amanuenses, one of whom provides a charming link between No. 10 and another house in the Square, No. 17. In 1761 the future Sir Philip Francis was a youth of twenty, but his skill in languages and his fine penmanship commended him to Pitt, who not only enjoyed dictating to him, but would even call upon the 'St Paul's boy' to give an opinion upon high affairs of State. Long afterwards, in her *Memoirs of Sir Philip Francis*, his widow mused that it was happy service at No. 10 (including many an hour of leisure in its library) which gave him a lifelong *tendresse* for the Square and influenced his choice of No. 17 as a retirement home.

In the case of Lord Derby, his grip on office during his three brief Premierships (1852, 1858–59, 1866–68) was too precarious to justify the upheaval of a transfer to Downing St. In any case this markedly self-sufficient grandee would

38. Sir Philip Francis. By J. Lonsdale.

probably have balked at living 'over the shop'. Official callers simply had to steer for No. 10 St James's Square, where he dwelt in somewhat shabby comfort ('the furnishings of a second-rate lodging house' snorted Disraeli, who expected glitter in his chief), and later for No. 33 during his second and third terms.

The Gladstone situation was quite different. All through the events which we have been describing – indeed from 1736 until 1890 – No. 10 was owned by the family of Heathcote (Hampshire baronets), who let it not only to miscellaneous statesmen but to Lady Blessington and the Windham Club (p. 106). By the time 1890 approached the old mansion was mortgaged to William Gladstone's wealthy elder brother, Sir Thomas. Gladstone himself, by no means opulent, had formed the habit of renting or borrowing a London house, just for the parliamentary session. The Heathcotes were supporters of his, and it is not clear whether he had to pay anyone for the use of No. 10. The counter-attraction of Downing St did not arise, since Gladstone's last period as Leader of the Opposition still had a couple of years to run, and only the adventures and misadventures of Parnell disturbed this interlude of comparative calm in the venerable statesman's life.

As soon as Gladstone moved out, the house was sold to the 11th Lord Kinnaird (December 1890) and he continued to occupy it until his death in 1923. Looking back to its period of greatest glory, it is only appropriate that it should then have become the nucleus of the Institute of International Affairs, under the evocative name of 'Chatham House' (p. 150).

* * *

A brief mention at least should be made of some other former residents in the Square who, if they never reached 'the top of the greasy pole' (in Disraeli's phrase), managed to shin a fair way up.

Apart from all those First Lords of the Treasury (who themselves of course held a variety of offices from time to time), St James's Square seems to have had a certain attraction for Lord Chancellors, including one or two of the most eminent. The list starts with John, 1st Lord Somers. One of William III's trusted supporters, he occupied the Woolsack between 1797 and 1701 and was resident at No. 21 in the latter year, when an unsuccessful attempt was made to impeach him. Then there is something of a gap until Henry 2nd Earl Bathurst, who as Lord Apsley was Lord Chancellor from 1771 to 78 and was the last member of his family to be associated with No. 20 before it was sold to the Williams Wynns in the 1770s. He was a buttoned-up sort of fellow, and when he had retired prudently to bed his nonogenarian father would exclaim 'Come, now the old gentleman's gone, let us crack another bottle!'

A more resounding name was that of Edward, 1st Lord Thurlow, twice Lord Chancellor (1778–83 and 1783–92). A thick-and-thin supporter of Lord North, he was nevertheless forced out of office by the latter during his brief coalition with Fox; Pitt restored him and he presided over the trial of Warren Hastings. Regarded as no less vulgar and arrogant than he was able, he was at No. 18 for some nine years (1794–1803), just in advance of the Castlereagh era. Almost immediately afterwards another ex-Lord Chancellor, Alexander Wedderburn, 1st Baron Loughborough and Earl of Rosslyn, descended on the Square. His stay at No. 12 was brief (1803–4), but he was succeeded there by his son James, who remained until 1826. James, though a soldier by profession, held Cabinet office of the honorific sort as Lord Privy Seal under Wellington (1829–30) and Lord President of the Council under Peel (1834–35). It was his grandson, the 4th Earl, who applied to Disraeli to be made Master of the Buckhounds (then a quasi-political office). 'I couldn't do that,' replied Dizzy. 'Your language would frighten the hounds. But if you like you can be Lord High Commissioner of the Church of Scotland.' And in the teeth of public opinion, Rosslyn got the job.

Foreign Secretaries (or their equivalent) also make quite an impressive showing. Chronicled elsewhere are the connections of Castlereagh with No. 18, the 5th Duke of Leeds with No. 21 and the 15th Earl of Derby with No. 33; to these may be added Edward, 2nd Viscount Conway, who as Secretary of State for the North occupied one of the houses on the site of No. 31 (1681–83).

Inevitably, the holders of strictly decorative office have abounded in such an aristocratic ambiance and are far too many to chronicle, but it is certainly a curiosity of our story that St James's Square has harboured at least seventeen Lords-Lieutenant of Ireland (rather more authentic than Dasent's fifteen 'Prime Ministers'!). Going round the Square we encounter the 3rd Lord Grantham, later Lord de Grey (No. 1 1806–30 and No. 4 1834–59), 3rd Earl of Hardwicke (No. 3 1801–34), 7th Earl Cowper (No. 4 1881–1905), 2nd Earl of Clarendon (No. 5 1676–79), 2nd Earl of Bristol (No. 6 1752–56, and later), the two Dukes of Ormonde (No. 9 between 1684 and 1715), 3rd Duke of Northumberland (No. 11 1818–22), 8th Earl of Pembroke, 13th Earl of Eglinton and 7th Duke of Marlborough (all at No. 12 in 1686–1733, 1846–58 and 1859–79 respectively), 1st Marquess of Bath (No. 15 1755), 1st Earl of Romney (No. 16 1691–1704), 4th Earl of Chesterfield (No. 18 1727–33), 1st Earl of Essex (No. 19 1677–83), 1st Duke of Dorset (No. 21 1718–23) and 2nd Duke of Bolton (No. 33 1702–07).

Resonant titles! But it cannot be said that – the Ormondes apart – the holders of any of them left a lasting mark, for good or ill, on the history of the island where they were sent to represent the British Crown.

X
Commerce Rears Its Head

So far, we have been considering St James's Square as essentially a congeries of private homes. The only exception was the Embassies, an important (though not always appreciated) element since the earliest days, but by the end of the eighteenth century almost extinct. 'Diplomatic privilege' invariably ruffles the temper of John Bull. In 1716–19, Signor Tron, Venetian Envoy, caused vexation by flatly refusing to pay rates on No. 19, and when at much the same period Ormonde House was let to the Marquis Monteleon, the Spanish Ambassador, it was later alleged that the house 'received more hurt than the Duke of Ormonde had done in twenty years . . . a foreign Minister never cares or minds what damage is done to the house he is in'.

No doubt it was with the Tron case in mind that the Act of 1726 stipulated (Clause V) that the Trustees' Rate on a house occupied by 'any Ambassador or Minister from any Foreign Prince or State' should be paid by the landlord or proprietor. As a rule ambassadorial tenancies were mercifully short, though we may note that early in the eighteenth century Ossulston House was occupied successively by representatives of Sweden, Venice, Savoy and Hanover, while Portugal, Prussia, France and Holland also made sporadic appearances elsewhere.

Ignoring the diplomats, it is possible to pinpoint the year 1796 as beginning a completely new phase in the social history of St James's Square, which to most of the inhabitants must have seemed at first an even more unwelcome aberration from the norm.

No. 8, on the east side of the Duke of York St corner, had not led a very glittering existence since Sir Mathew Decker's death in 1749. In the usual St James's Square fashion, his dowager stayed on for a decade or so, then, in the 1760s, the house was let to Viscount Fitzwilliam. Finally, in 1768, Lady Decker's executors sold it to Sir Sampson Gideon, son of a very rich Portuguese stock-broker. The parental wealth had secured him a baronetcy at the tender age of fourteen and he had perhaps accelerated his rise in the world by marrying the daughter of Sir John Eardley-Wilmot, Chief Justice of Common Pleas. Nor did his Jewish-Portuguese origins deter William Pitt from including him in a huge clutch of appointments to the Irish peerage in 1789, though the new Baron Eardley of Spalding continued to represent various rotten boroughs in the House of Commons for some years after that.

As soon as he bought No. 8, Gideon commissioned extensive alterations by the firm of Henry Holland, including the transfer of the front entrance from the Square into Duke of York St. However in 1784 he moved out and for the next twelve years the house apparently stood empty, the Square Rate being paid by shadowy figures such as 'Mathias de Gandesque (landlord)', or 'the assignees of Freeman & Grace'.

At long last, in the year 1796 aforesaid, appeared the name of 'Josiah Wedgwood Esq.'. Here was another second-generation man, son of the world's most famous potter and now the head of the firm. He had paid £8500 for No. 8 and was evidently prepared to spend a lot more on adapting it as his West End showroom – the very first incursion of commerce into the Square, if one ignores one or two squalid little enterprises on the South side.

Tradition has it that the Wedgwood initiative raised a storm of resentment among the highborn residents on the East, North and West. If so, it found no echo in the Trust's proceedings, at any rate as recorded in its Minutes; the members must have been sadly aware that there was nothing in their Act of Parliament to prevent a development which was simply beyond the imaginings of 1726. What we do know is that the Trustees had no qualms about taking Mr Wedgwood's money, and between 1796 and 1829 he figures regularly in the Rate book, either alone or in conjunction with Thomas Byerley, his cousin and first manager.

The decision to set up shop in St James's Square has been regarded as a deliberate act of snobbery by Josiah junr, whose father's successive London showrooms had been in somewhat less glamorous Newport St, St Martin's Lane, and Greek Street, Soho, where he paid a rent of no more than £200 a year.

None of old Josiah's three sons was a committed potter, as the most recent writers on the family[1] make clear. John, the eldest, aspired to banking, with damaging results; Thomas, the youngest, was an intellectual, with strong scientific and literary leanings; while Josiah junr's main aspiration was to the dignity of a country landowner, first in Surrey and later further West. For all three, the idea of a mansion in St James's Square which could be used as a centre for London entertaining as well as for business premises, had a strong appeal.

In itself, No. 8 was not unsuitable for either rôle. The early Wedgwood historian, Mrs Meteyard, describes it as extremely large, the rooms noble and

39. *Josiah Wedgwood jnr. By William Owen.*

lofty, the staircases wide and the cellarage 'on a scale to accommodate the wares of Brobdingnag'. The trouble was that St James's Square was inconvenient for the trade and too quiet a nook to attract shoppers of the window-gazing order. Josiah senr had set great store by having plenty of room for 'my ladys', who often

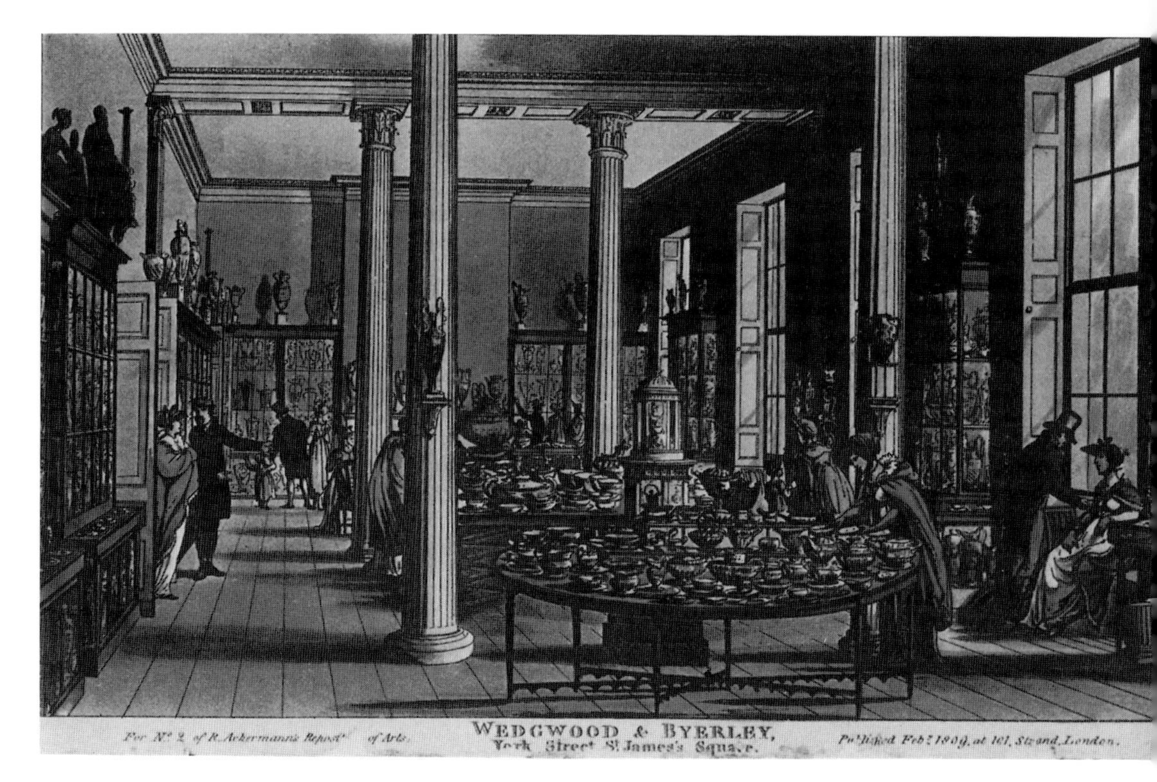

40. No. 8 as Wedgwood showroom, 1796–1829.

came in 'large shoals together', but at No. 8 dead stock was more prevalent than live customers. Moreover, the young Wedgwoods were soon to discover that their aristocratic neighbours tended to be bad payers – the fact that the Marquess of Donegal at No. 3 had not settled a bill for fifteen years did not deter him from ordering further goods or the firm from supplying them. When Thomas Byerley, a hopelessly inefficient manager, died in 1811 it was discovered that accounts outstanding amounted to no less than £41,477 – greater than the total assets of the business.

The end came, so far as No. 8 was concerned, in 1828. It was decided to close the showrooms and sell off the stock; the sale lasted for months, and though it formed the basis for many a famous collection in the future, it is significant that not a single member of the Wedgwood family bought anything. However, it was some satisfaction that the house itself fetched £16,000 – almost twice what Josiah junr had paid for it.

A secondary, but even less fortunate, link between the Wedgwoods and the Square had been broken much earlier. Within two years of the opening of the showroom, a banker called Alexander Davison had moved into No. 11, a few doors away. One might have assumed that it was this propinquity which led to John Wedgwood becoming a partner in the firm of Davison & Co. (later to be known by the inordinate title of 'Davison, Noel, Templer, Middleton, Johnson & Wedgwood'), but the connection seems to have been formed in Josiah senr's day.

In any case, it proved uniformly disastrous, and the business was only saved from insolvency by being taken over by Messrs Coutts in 1816.

The following year Alexander Davison himself (usually known to posterity as Nelson's Prize Agent) vanished from No. 11, to be succeeded by Hugh Percy, 3rd Duke of Northumberland, no less.

As to No. 8, it was no doubt to the relief of the neighbours that, with the Wedgwoods gone, they saw it too sink back into the arms of the peerage, in the person of Charles Marsham, 3rd Earl of Romney of the 2nd creation, scion of a Civil Service family and unconnected with him of the fireworks. The reprieve, however, was but temporary; by 1840 No. 8 had been engulfed in the next wave of intruders, the Clubs – of that, more in the next chapter.

* * *

It took commerce only four years after the Wedgwood retreat to re-establish a salient in St James's Square. In 1844, what was then called the London & Westminster Bank bought No. 1 from the 4th Earl of Dartmouth. A pleasant recent publication[2] reminds us that this concern had been the first to take advantage of the 1833 legislation which, in the teeth of the Bank of England and the private bankers, authorized joint-stock banks to establish branches. On March 10 1834 the London & Westminster opened simultaneously a head office in Throgmorton St and a West End branch at 9 Waterloo Place. This soon proved too small. The directors, seeking an alternative, lit on No. 1 St James's Square, which had been empty for over a year, Lord Dartmouth having moved across Charles II St into what later became known as Derby House (No. 33). The Bank paid £10,000 for No. 1, to serve both as business premises and as a residence for the manager, Mr Vile – bankers were often expected to 'live in' in those days.

No. 1, it will be recalled, was one of two houses built on the site of the old Ossulston House, when it was demolished in 1754. The other was occupied by the Boscawens, Viscounts Falmouth, and it is rather pleasing to contemplate the two estuarial dynasties settling down side by side. No. 1 had been bought on behalf of William Legge, 2nd Earl of Dartmouth, who had recently got married. So the Legges altogether owned No. 1 for 87 years, though for a substantial portion of that time it was let to a member of another great St James's Square clan, Thomas Weddell (later de Grey), 3rd Baron Grantham and eventual inheritor of No. 4.

From 1844 to the present day, No. 1 has flourished as a Bank. Amalgamations changed its title in turn to the 'London County & Westminster' and then to the 'London County Westminster & Parr's Bank' of one's childhood, shortened in 1923 to the 'Westminster'. A final and spectacular amalgamation produced the 'National Westminster' in January 1970; by a happy coincidence it brought together the venerable branch at No. 1 with that established by the National Provincial across the way at No. 33 in 1942. The vicissitudes of these concerns during and after the World War II 'blitz' will be a theme of Chap. XIII.

Wedgwoods, of course, had chosen the North side of the Square and the London & Westminster the East, so that there was a certain symmetry in the Square's third business enterprise establishing itself on the Western perimeter.

The Anson family, proud of the grand Grecian house created for them by James Stuart and Samuel Wyatt, were always free spenders and it was for this reason no doubt that they let No. 15 more than they lived in it. The imposing list of tenants begins with Sir Henry Vane-Tempest and his wife, the Countess of Antrim. They were there in 1800–2, and their famous daughter, Frances Anne, Marchioness of Londonderry, records in her memoirs that she was born in the house. Later came the Duchess of Gordon, the Marquess of Abercorn, Lord Ellenborough (Lord Chief Justice), the 2nd Earl Grey (Prime Minister) and finally the Duke of Bedford (1821–29). Nearly all these grandees were related to the Ansons in one degree or another.

It was the accession of George, 2nd Viscount Anson and 1st Earl of Lichfield, that ended this particular St James's Square dynasty. The Turf was his pet extravagance, and though during his reign from 1820 onwards he intermittently occupied No. 15, for the most part it continued to be rented, latterly by Clubs – the Army & Navy from 1846 to 1850, and the Junior United Service while its own clubhouse in Charles II St was being rebuilt in 1855.

Long before that, Lord Lichfield had made his first attempt to sell out. We have lively evidence for this in the 'Particulars and Conditions of Sale' issued in 1842 by George Robins, a copy of which happily survives.[3] Robins was a famous 'puffer', as readers of Surtees will no doubt recall, but the auction on April 30 flopped. The sale of furniture, which occupied six days in June, seems to have gone better. Then in May 1855 Christie's took a hand with even more elaborate Particulars, but again the 'Princely Habitation' failed to find a purchaser.

Next Lord Lichfield tried to unload his splendid incubus onto a property speculator called William Sedgwick, of Regent St, who the following year agreed to buy it for £15,300, but unfortunately went broke at the critical moment. So at last No. 15 St James's Square, which is reputed to have cost Thomas Anson the First £60,000, was sold for only £12,750 to the Clerical, Medical and General Life Assurance Society, which is still in possession. Dasent records, with just surprise, that this was probably 'the cheapest transfer of freehold property' in the Square in recent times.

Tenants at first of the Duke of Bedford at various Bloomsbury addresses, the directors of the Society had looked at several houses in and around St James's Square, once the decision to move west had been taken. The old Adair mansion on the South side was tempting for a time; No. 8 (then the Erectheum Club) needed too many alterations; No. 2 was too dark. Eventually, in April 1856, the No. 15 deal was consummated.

At that date the Society was already 32 years old, but still a comparative youngster among English life assurance companies of the period. As its somewhat cumbrous title still recalls, it intended to find many of its assurers among

PARTICULARS AND CONDITIONS OF SALE

OF

THE DISTINGUISHED

FREEHOLD MANSION,

For a lengthened period

THE FAVOURED HABITATION OF

THE RIGHT HON.

The EARL OF LICHFIELD

Situated on the West and preferable side of

ST. JAMES' SQUARE,

Being No. 13, and extending into Duke Street. It is really altogether, from its size and importance,

A Princely Habitation,

WITH

A MAGNIFICENT & IMPOSING STONE FRONT,

Embellished with elegant

IONIC STONE COLUMNS.

On the Ground and principal Floors are

GRAND SUITES OF

FIVE ELEGANT AND SPACIOUS ROOMS;

And the Mansion throughout is complete in each department. Communicating with the Mansion by

A COURT YARD,

IS A

TWELVE-STALL STABLE

AND

STANDING FOR FIVE CARRIAGES,

With numerous appurtenances;

Which will be Sold by Auction, by

Mr. GEO. ROBINS,

AT THE AUCTION MART,

On THURSDAY, the 28th Day of APRIL, 1842, at Twelve,

WITH IMMEDIATE POSSESSION.

Particulars can be had of Edward White, Esq., 12, Great Marlborough Street; Messrs. Vizard and Leman, 51, Lincoln's Inn Fields; at the Mansion; the Auction Mart; and at Mr. GEORGE ROBINS' Offices, Covent Garden.

SMITH & ROBINS, Printers, King Street, Long Acre.

41. *No. 15 – George Robins's 'Particulars of Sale', 1842.*

two professional classes – parsons, because they were presumably reliable characters who led virtuous lives; doctors, because they would know how to look after themselves (not actuarily correct, as a matter of fact). What is more, it was proposed to have a predominance of clergy and medical men on the Board of Management. There were more of the latter than the former, as it turned out, though one unconquerable cleric, Prebendary Kempe, Rector of St James's Piccadilly, sat on the board for over fifty years. He was still signing cheques with enthusiasm within a few weeks of his death in 1907, when he was 97 years of age. Quite a number of directors and executives set a good example to their assurers (though not to their annuitants) by living and working into a robust old age, as we know from A. D. Besant's *Our Centenary*,[4] perhaps the only book on life assurance which can be read for laughs.

As might be expected, the Clerical, Medical, along with the London Library (p. 111), took the lead in opposition to what looked like a harmless enough reform by the Metropolitan Board of Works in 1884. This was a re-numbering, consequent upon the present Nos. 8 and 9 being incorporated in the Square instead of, as heretofore, in Duke of York St. Everyone from No. 8 onwards was of course affected, but the Clerical, Medical and the Library felt that (in contrast to the private residents) they had a specific grievance; the former would have to trace and contact the holders of over 10,000 'Policies of Assurance' – as it was, it often received letters sent to addresses it had quit forty years or more ago; the latter would not only have to notify its subscribers, but to re-label some 100,000 volumes 'on the outside and again on the inside'. The clubs, with problems of their own, lent their support, as did most of the private residents, though the Duke of Norfolk and Lord Derby (who probably did not accept that their mansions had numbers at all) seem to have held aloof.

Alas, the majestic MEMORIAL[5] sent to the Board of Works failed to change the decision, and it was left to the East India Club (relegated from 14 to 16) to signalize its displeasure by refusing to inscribe the new number on its doorposts for another twenty-two years.

In spite of having to make many interior adaptations at No. 15, the Clerical, Medical has remained the sensitive guardian of its heritage, a task which has been eased by the transference of the greater part of the head office business elsewhere.

I *No. 15: The Staircase Dome – decoration by James Stuart or Samuel Wyatt.*

II *No. 20: Ceiling of Lady Wynn's dressing-room by Robert Adam.*

III *St James's Square Garden, 1941.*

Auxiliary Fire Service digging for victory. (Note the Statue of King William III removed for safe keeping and the railings for scrap.)

St James's Square

Painting by Adrian Allington commissioned under the War Artists' Advisory Scheme and now the property of Westminster City Libraries.

IV *Garden in winter.*

V *Garden in summer.*

XI

. . . And then the Clubs

Rather surprisingly, some seventy years passed before commerce extended its bridgehead in St James's Square, but well in advance of Wedgwood's withdrawal another important non-private element had made its first incursion. This was the clubs. Leading the field came the Union, and though it was to have a dignified later history, its 21 St James's Square phase (1807–16) was on the whole deleterious.

The Union had been founded in 1799, with a whiggish membership which included Sheridan, Charles James Fox, Sir Francis Burdett and the Dukes of Bedford and Norfolk. In 1807 it migrated from Cumberland House, Pall Mall, to St James's Square under the management of George Raggett (later associated with White's), and while not precisely a gambling 'hell' in, say, the Crockford's sense, it quickly became known for exceedingly high play. Among those whom this attracted were Lord Byron (he signed on in 1810), along with his little circle of close cronies, Henry Hobhouse, Douglas Kinnaird and Scrope Davies.[1] St James's Square seems such a natural ambiance for the young Byron, quite apart from his nights at the Union, that a little diversion in pursuit of him there may be pardoned. For example, we hear of him attending private theatricals at No. 3 (Lord Hardwicke's) in the company of the two exiled French princes, the Duc du Berri and the Duc d'Angoulême; in verse, he celebrates Mrs Boehm's masked balls[2] at No. 16 (more about Mrs Boehm shortly); while in prose we have his own spirited account of an evening in November 1813:

> Sunday, I dined with Lord Holland in St. James's Square. Large party – among them Sir S[amuel] Romilly and . . . Lord John Russell, and others, 'good men and true'. Stuffed myself with sturgeon, and exceeded in champagne and wine in general, but not to confusion of head . . . Why does Lady Holland always have that damned screen between the whole room and the fire? I, who bear cold no better than an antelope . . . was absolutely petrified, and could not even shiver. All the rest, too, looked as if they were just unpacked, like salmon from an ice-basket, and set down to table for that day only . . .[3]

Finally, a strange and even sinister Byronic echo, long after his death at Missolonghi in 1824. Between 1832 and 1845, No. 12 was owned by the 8th Lord King, later Earl of Lovelace, in fact it was he who had the house rebuilt by Thomas Cubitt. King was married to Byron's daughter Ada, whose mother, Arabella Lady Byron, had rescued from unhappy exile in France Byron's other daughter Medora, supposed offspring of his liaison with his half-sister Augusta Leigh. Writing to Lady Byron from No. 12 one day in July 1842, Medora exclaims,

> I have this instant met my Mother. She was crossing the Square coming from York St, as the carriage drove up to the door. I instantly recognised her – she is unchanged in face – and turned my head as if waiting for William, who was ringing at the door. She could not have seen my face – my veil being down . . . she had reached the Duke of Cleveland's before I got out . . . She was followed by a dirty-looking rascally kind of servant out of livery who was playing with his glove . . . Her large eyes are indeed *unchanged*, her walk most altered, she shuffles along as if she tried to carry the ground she walks on, and she looks WICKED . . .[4]

* * *

Reverting for a moment to the Union, towards the end of its time in St James's Square it proved fatal to at least one member of the Byronic circle, Scrope Davies. He had won large sums there, including an occasion when, having left a convivial gathering with Byron, Hobhouse and others and gone to bed, he got up again, made for the Union and finished £3700 to the good. But soon afterwards came a night when he lost £150, then threw away his whole fortune trying to recoup it.

A much more respectable successor to the Union was the Windham, formerly known as the Windham House Club and named from the home of the politician William Windham in Pall Mall, which it had briefly occupied before moving to No. 10 St James's Square in 1829.

42. George Gordon, 6th Lord Byron. By R. Westall.

No. 10 was then, so to speak, between Prime Ministers – the elder Pitt had long gone, Stanley and Gladstone were still over the horizon – but it had been enjoying a brilliant phase through the tenancy of the 'gorgeous' Countess of Blessington, now (along with her complaisant husband) at the start of her social career. Blessington, an Irish peer with a rent-roll of £30,000, took a long lease of

No. 10, and spent a mint of money fitting it out in a suitably ostentatious style, though Carrington[5] doubts the *scale* of their entertaining in view of the comparatively modest size of the house. In any case, the Blessingtons had only been three or four years in possession before the celebrated *menage à trois* with Count d'Orsay developed, and sent her ladyship on a prolonged tour abroad. She never again lived permanently in St James's Square; Seamore Place in Mayfair and Gore House, Kensington, were her future theatres of operation. Blessington himself died in 1829 and his widow, who had been paying the owners, the Heathcotes, a rent of £840 per annum, let No. 10 furnished to the Windham Club at a handsome £1350.

This arrangement came to an end in 1836, when the club moved to a more permanent home three doors away. No. 13, built and owned by the Clarges family (p. 5), resembled No. 10 in not being a mansion of conspicuous size or grandeur, but it had a magical attraction for Dukes, no fewer than nine, of various families, having owned or briefly rented it.[6] Of these by far the most interesting was John Ker, 3rd Duke of Roxburgh, the great bibliophile. He lived in the house for only nine years (1795–1804), but a dispute over the dukedom held up the intended dispersal of his collection until 1812, when the auction by Evans of Pall Mall was spread over 42 days. In the circumstances, the total yield of £23,241 seems fairly moderate, even in 1812 money.

Dasent reports that when the Windham arrived in 1836, some of the ducal bookcases were still there, and were in use in his own time. He could speak from experience, since he was himself a Windham member, and no doubt much collating of the great heap of information he brought together for his *History* was done in the Club library during the 1890s. At its foundation, the Windham was supposed to have literary leanings, though whether these were perpetuated, says Dasent rather drily, 'it is not for us to enquire'. He pays more heartfelt tribute to the club's kitchen and cellar, and mentions the interesting detail that it was the first in London to open its doors to strangers.

Surviving members of the Windham testify to its quiet and pleasant social atmosphere and continued to lament its loss after it closed in 1940.[7]

Next on the list as a home of clubs is undoubtedly No. 8, which sheltered as many as six between the departure of Lord Romney (p. 99) and the end of the century. Most of them were totally ephemeral and need not detain us, though the Erectheum (1840–54), like the Windham, had a faintly literary reputation. When the Sports took over in 1893 there was no reason to suppose it would be any more durable, especially as its promoter, the Corinthian baronet Sir John Astley, had already been associated with at least two clubs which had flopped. Yet the Sports persisted and flourished, occupying No. 8 until amalgamation with the East India in 1938.

The story of this most friendly and convivial of clubs has been given to the world quite recently,[8] while that of the ebullient athlete who created it was told long ago in his zestful *Autobiography*. It may be mentioned that the smoking-room extension towards Duke of York Street was believed to represent the dimensions of the Chapel which formerly stood there, the billiard-room below replacing its crypt. Built when No. 8 was the French Embassy (p. 73), it was briefly converted to secular uses by Josiah Wedgwood, but between 1799 and 1833 became a place of worship once more, sheltering in turn Swedenborgians, Baptists, Unitarians and finally the fashionable Anglican preacher, Stopford Brooke.

Throughout its occupation of No. 8, the Sports was confronted across Duke of York St by the Portland Club, famous arbiter of card games, which in 1887 had taken over from the Hoare family of bankers, owners since as far back as 1790; their ultimate representative was Mrs Anne Hoare – notable as the Square's only recorded centenarian. The Portland remained in possession of No. 9 till 1943. It even built itself a nice little oriel window to improve the lighting of its billiard-room, but this has since disappeared.

None of these houses shelters a club today – that privilege rests with No. 16. But long before it became part of clubland it had become part of history. Lady Betty Germain's old mansion was bought in 1785 for £3500[9] by the Ansons of No. 15, who pulled it down with the intention of enlarging their own domain. Eventually, however, a new house was built on the site by a West India merchant of Russian origin called Edmund Boehm. He had an ambitious wife, whose social career was destined to reach its climax and almost its full-stop on the evening of June 21 1815, when the Prince Regent himself was among her guests.

How many chroniclers have described the moment when a coach, diverted from Lord Castlereagh's mansion, dashed up to No. 16 and disgorged Major Henry Percy, bearing four French eagles and Wellington's Waterloo Dispatch! Dancing, about to begin, was forgotten. His Royal Highness withdrew into another room (probably the present Club library) to hear the dispatch read, then emerged to announce the news. What is not so often recorded is that instead of uttering cries of triumph, many of those present (including the Regent) shed tears at the loss of so many young lives, and the party dispersed in silence. Mrs Boehm's reaction was different. Long after her husband's bankruptcy and death she was still nursing her grievance against the Battle of Waterloo – why could they not have kept back the news and saved her ball from ruin?[10]

After the débâcle of the Boehms, No. 16 was sold first to a Mr Robert Vyner and then to the wealthy Irish peer, the Marquess of Clanricarde. He seems to have used it as his town house for about twenty years, but between 1846 and 1849 let it successively to two of the many here-today-and-gone-tomorrow clubs of the mid-century – the Prince of Wales and the Free Trade.

The house was conveniently vacant again by the time the recently formed East India Club was in search of a rooftree. There was already one eminent club, the Oriental (then in Hanover Square), which catered – though not exclusively – for the Company's servants, but a section now opted for complete self-containment. A deciding factor may well have been the alleged grudging attitude of the

43. The East India Club façade by Charles Fish, 1864.

Oriental to officers on furlough, though strangely enough proposals for fusion with the older body were explored more than once in the early days.

The East India held its inaugural dinner on January 1 1850, but within three years found itself decidedly cramped for space. The tale of its attempts to expand – not without comedy and confusion – can be followed in the earlier chapters of *Foursome in St James's*. They lasted for years; in relation to the Square, however, they only became significant when, after fruitless negotiations with Mr Sedgwick (p. 100) about No. 15, the committee finally turned its gaze southwards and in 1863 agreed to buy No. 17[11] for £14,500. As it had just agreed also to pay Lord Clanricarde £1500 more than that for the freehold of No. 16, it was now in a position to house itself in a manner befitting a confederacy of officers and gentlemen.

It did so by retaining the Clanricarde house (including Mrs Boehm's historic apartments), but demolishing No. 17, substituting for it a spacious coffee-room with an equally monumental drawing-room above it, and throwing across the whole a unifying façade. Grand enough in its proportions, connoisseurs have always been sniffy about its architectural details. Who was responsible? 'Charles Lee' has until recently been the universal answer; echo now replies 'Charles Fish'. Mr Lee (better known as a surveyor in large practice than as an architect) was certainly involved up to the last minute, but research has revealed that it was Mr Fish, a builder in Pimlico, who was finally invited to 'prepare an elevation'.

It may be that the club would have got something a little more prestigious if an earlier move to bring in Decimus Burton (of the Athenaeum, the Hyde Park Corner Screen, *et al.*) had been successful. Yet the passer-by must admit that Mr Fish's creation, as carefully restored in 1984–85 and given a shining livery of cream-and-white paint with blue trimmings, adds a certain splendour to the north-west segment of the Square.

The later history of the club is mainly a record of successful amalgamations, as symbolized by its present full title – the East India, Devonshire, Sports and Public Schools Club, but that is not of immediate concern.

Also very much with us is that famous institution, the Army & Navy Club, universally known as the 'Rag'.[12] Physically, its relationship with the Square has been and remains anomalous. On the one hand, the Trust records it under the number 22, and its entrance is in the little slip (once known as George St) leading from the south-west corner of the Square into Pall Mall; on the other, it has always had an important façade on the great 'street of clubs' and its postal address is actually 36–9 Pall Mall. What is beyond doubt is its record of loyalty to the Square; it has faithfully paid the Statutory and Voluntary Rates and its Secretaries are nowadays numbered among the Trustees.

For over a century, the Rag was even more conspicuous than the East India, for size and architectural assertiveness. After temporary sojourns at No. 18 (p. 120) and No. 12 between 1837 and 1850, the Club went through torments of indecision (well chronicled by Capt. Firebrace and the *Survey*) before making up its mind who should design its permanent home. Along the way, two Gothic confections by George Truefitt and Gilbert Scott respectively and a Moorish one by Owen Jones were perhaps mercifully rejected. What finally emerged was an enormous palazzo in the Venetian style, designed by Messrs C. O. Parnell & A. Smith. Described by Dasent as 'a happy combination of Sansovino's Palazzo Cornaro . . . and St Mark's Library', but with three open arches on the entrance front recalling Somerset House, this architectural heavyweight cost all of £54,000, exclusive of foundation work and furnishings.

A more detailed account of the Parnell & Smith building would be otiose, since it was torn down in 1962 and replaced by the present strictly twentieth-century structure by Messrs T. P. Bennett. But it must be noted that to make

44. The Army & Navy Club. Parnell & Smith, 1851. Demolished 1962.

room for Parnell & Smith the club itself had to acquire and demolish the interesting house to which we have given the number '21a' (p. 8), the site of which is, incidentally, the only part of the 'Rag' recognized by Dasent as belonging to the Square. In its later days it had been the property of the Hon. William Ponsonby (Lord de Mauley from 1838), though one more ephemeral club, the Parthenon, occupied it between 1837 and 1841. Lord de Mauley and his mortgagees did rather well out of '21a', considering that they had bought it from Samuel Thornton for £11,000 and got £19,500 10*s* when they sold it to the 'Rag', merely for demolition.

The late nineteenth century represented the apogee of the Square as a province of 'clubland'; since then there have been far more losses than gains – only a couple of substantial, if temporary, gains in fact, when the British Empire Club (successor to a couple of ephemera) occupied No. 12 from 1909 to 1942[14] and the Caledonian 32 and part of 33 between 1922 and the blitz. Today the East India and the 'Rag' are the sole survivors.

The relationship of the various clubs with the Square – hingeing largely on the

45. Thomas Carlyle. By J. E. Boehm.

great question of 'keys to the garden'! – will be explored in a later chapter. But perhaps this is an appropriate place to introduce another early intruder which had and has some of the genial characteristics of a club, though belonging more exactly to the category of 'institutions'. This is the London Library, which as long ago as 1845 took a lease of No. 14, acquiring the freehold thirty-four years later. From what we know of its then size and condition (p. 43), the price paid, £21,000, seems pretty steep, though its narrow frontage concealed much scope for expansion, full advantage of which has been taken since. In 1845, No. 14 was sometimes known as 'Beauchamp House', from the occupancy of the Lygon family – William, 1st Earl Beauchamp (1799–1816), and then, during her long widowhood, Katherine, Countess Beauchamp (1817–44).

The founder of the London Library – one might almost say its patron saint – was Thomas Carlyle. Moved in part by his dislike of the British Museum, and in particular of its librarian, Panizzi, he canvassed his friends, with the result that at a meeting held at the Freemasons' Tavern in June 1840, it was decided that a subscription library, designed essentially to lend out books to the literary world, was urgently needed and that a committee should be formed to promote it. Carlyle said he was too busy to serve, but he was not sparing of advice. Characteristic sample – when asked whether the Marquess of Northampton should be offered the presidency, he replied, 'Any lord will do – it is a mere ensign'. The Earl of Clarendon was subsequently chosen.

Leaving aside ornamental peers, it was typical of the Library from that day to this that the sub-committee which found its original home, the 1st floor of No. 7 Pall Mall, and carefully checked the chimneys and drains, consisted of Mr W. E. Gladstone and Sir Edward Bunbury, with W. M. Thackeray as auditor. It was Gladstone again who eventually advised the purchase of the freehold of No. 14. The Pall Mall premises soon became unbearably cramped and the move to St James's Square must have been greeted with enormous relief.

There is perhaps no institution in the world quite like the 'LL'. A dwindling number of subscription libraries may survive, but there can be no other where it is possible to browse at large among perhaps a million volumes, and where the rules are so liberally framed that members seem sometimes to have drifted dreamily along under the impression that they could take out as many books as they liked and keep them for ever. 'A permanent anachronism' was the apt phrase used by one contributor to the London Library's own anthology of tributes by grateful readers,[15] and there is certainly something pleasingly out of date about the interior, with its solid wooden fittings, roomy staircase, rows of heavy catalogues (no 'Dewey classification' here) and above all the delightful L-shaped reading-room overlooking the Square, where books are not just read – they are written.[16]

No wonder the Library has been associated with so many resonant names in English letters – Carlyle and Thackeray as already mentioned, followed by Dickens and Herbert Spencer and most of the great Victorians and their successors, with perhaps a particular floraison in the period of Aldous Huxley, Rose Macaulay, E. M. Forster, Harold Nicolson and the Sitwells. No wonder, too, that there was an outburst of loyalty when the Library suffered heavily by losing its rating appeal in the 1950s,[17] and autograph MSS and other treasures flooded in for a sale at Christie's in June 1960 which raised no less than £25,000. Fictional characters, it may be added, from Dr Watson to James Bond and George Smiley, are among those who have made urgent use of its resources.

Architecturally, the contribution of No. 14 to the fair face of St James's Square is not perhaps quite as distinguished as it would have been had Robert Adam's scheme (p. 44) been carried out. The architect for the rebuilding in 1896–98 was J. Osborne Smith and the result is amiable, though slightly baffling – Elizabethan motifs here, Georgian there, and even the faint flavour of a twentieth-century 'grid'.

Mention of the latter reminds us that the bookstacks in some of the numerous back and side extensions are floored with metal grills, which give a haunting resonance and through which pencils and biros disappear down, down . . .

XII
Victorian Heyday

'The Bishop of London is actually sitting on my left hand talking about the weather and Dutch fleet and a multitude of foreign fowls from Brooks' Menagerie which are sent into our Square for their health, and left there screaming and starving all day and night, and the Bishop assures me that this violation of decorum is connived at by the Duke of Norfolk, who pockets 6*d* a week for these cursed bipeds which, not having a feather left, look very like christians in adversity . . .' So wrote Sir Philip Francis to Lady Thanet on April 19 1804.[1] A strange tale, since at that date of course there was no garden – just the open pavé with the railing and basin in the middle; it is interesting to speculate on how the 'screaming and starving' creatures were accommodated and, for that matter, by what right the Duke was levying his 6*d* per week.

It seemed at first sight that this sharp little cameo by the reputed 'Junius' might be a unique example of a letter penned while a Trustees' meeting was in full swing, but the Minute Book shows that it was on Friday the 27th that they convened. This in itself raises a further question, because Francis continues:

> The Bishop of London[2] and I are to have a meeting on special affairs on the 27th inst. to which the Duke of Norfolk and the Earl of Rosslyn are invited, to see whether any means can be devised to prevent the future beating of carpets in this Tetragon. The base practise is patronised by George Byng, who says he doesn't choose to trust his carpets out of his sight. *En attendant*, we have the full and undivided benefit of the dust in all the carpets within 2 miles of us. . .

So it appears that if Francis's 'special meeting' did take place, he had got its proposed date mixed up with that of the full session, for which it was clearly intended to prepare the ground. In any case, the result was a triumphant resolution:

> That no carpets be allowed to be beat in the Square but those belonging to the inhabitants of the East, North and West sides, and those only in the months of August and September [when of course no self-respecting Trustee would be seen in Town].

This was by no means their first wrestle with the grave question of carpet beating. Already by May 17 1728 we find the Trustees stipulating that no carpets must be hung (and presumably beaten) around the Basin, and in May 1766 Mr Adair (South side) is refused permission to beat his – if such a 'liberty' were granted him it would soon be claimed by everyone.

Whether or not the conclave of the Bishop, the Duke, the Earl and Sir Philip actually occurred, that episode throws into relief one of the most striking facts about the St James Square Trust – the contrast between the grandeur of the persons involved (and in that age they were very grand indeed) and the homeliness of the concerns to which they bent their minds. When we read (as late as June 1873) of the 15th Earl of Derby being told off, along with the 3rd Marquess of Bristol, to 'mark out sites for planting some additional trees in the Garden', it seems a humble assignment enough on the eve of his second term as Disraeli's Foreign Secretary. Yet the tradition has continued until today, now that the representatives of great corporations have taken over from those of the House of Lords.

Of course, as with every voluntary organization under heaven, the drudgery was shouldered by a small core of devotees. This was particularly marked during the rather drowsy epoch of the mid-nineteenth century. Oddly enough, we hardly ever know how many Trustees there were at any one time – a browse through the new Minute Book inaugurated in 1833 reveals that during the ensuing twenty-five years the average attendance was just under six, with some twenty-three Trustees showing up at least once. But there were extremely few 'regulars'. Easily at the top came Lord de Grey (No. 4) (23 meetings), Bishop Sumner (No. 21) (22 meetings), Mr Wilbraham Egerton and his son, the future Lord Egerton of Tatton (No. 9) (21 meetings). Nobody else got into double figures except the 2nd Marquess of Bristol (No. 7) (11 meetings, mostly in the years immediately preceding his death in 1859). Moreover there were leading families and long-term residents in the Square who kept aloof for long periods. There is no record of any of the Ansons, subsequently Earls of Lichfield (No. 15), adorning a meeting of Trustees later than the end of the eighteenth century; the Williams Wynn baronets at No. 20 hardly ever appeared after the death of our original Sir Watkin's son in 1840, while the fashionable ex-Quaker Hudson Gurney, did so only twice during his forty-one years at No. 11 (1823–64). Some houses seem to have been rather more Trust-orientated than others; an example is No. 12 where, in addition to Lord Rosslyn, the Earls of Lovelace and Eglinton

& Winton, followed by the 7th Duke of Marlborough, played a modest but consistent part during the nineteenth century.

All this was long before the formal appointment of a Chairman, though in practice one enthusiast would often take charge for a long spell and be occasionally referred to as the 'managing Trustee' (he signed cheques). From about 1830 onwards, this tended to be Lord de Grey; after his death in the same year as Lord Bristol, Bishop Sumner (probably the busiest man in the Square) presided almost non-stop until his retirement in 1869. Subsequently Lord Derby and Lord Egerton of Tatton played Box and Cox up to the end of the century, the former being in fact the only Trustee present at the 1889, 1890 and 1891 AGMs!

By then, admittedly, the Trustees' field of action had greatly shrunk. When they first convened in 1726, everything that went on in the Square was under their control – law and order, paving, lighting, scavenging (the inhabitants were specifically exempted from the parochial Scavenging Rate), the operations of hackney cabmen and much else. We have already seen the old-time watchmen swept away by the 1831 Police Act, and at their May 1856 meeting the Trustees were informed that under the new Metropolitan Local Management Act, the 'repair, cleaning etc. of the carriage way and footpaths' would be looked after by the Paving Committee of the St James's Vestry.

A couple of 'grey areas' remained. Firstly, the Vestry tried to disclaim responsibility for the footway round the outside of the garden enclosure; the Trustees resisted and the vestrymen passed a somewhat absurd face-saving resolution – they would do the job, but without waiving their right to make the Trustees do it. The Vestry then said it expected them to continue looking after the eight lamps on the railing. This again the Trustees disputed and though the outcome of the argument is not minuted, it is fairly clear that soon lighting also devolved upon the local authority.

The most tangible result of all this was, for the residents, a slashing of the Square Rate from 7*s* per foot of frontage in 1855 to only 1*s* 6*d* the following year. By contrast, of course, the Vestry's own rate (a much more onerous matter) moved sharply upward. Dasent, who painstakingly records the parish rates at 20-year intervals, shows that whereas, for example, George Byng was paying only £53 per annum on No. 5 in 1836, this had jumped to £90 by 1856 (trimmed somewhat later on). For a specimen of 1986 rating, see note 17 on p. 166, col. 1!

The switch from private to public control did not necessarily mean that things were managed any better. As late as 1888 a member of the East India Club Committee proposed that the club itself should hire a crossing-sweeper to look after their own segment of the Square, but this was turned down as a bit *too* anachronistic.

The Trustees' loss of authority outside the garden enclosure was signalled in 1860, when they evidently felt that they could not veto the erection of a Cabmen's Shelter on the South side; the most they could do was to seek an

St. James's Square Trust
5th July 1878. } At a Meeting of the Trustees of St. James's Square, held this day at the residence of Lord Egerton of Tatton, No. 7, in the Square

Present – The Marquis of Bristol in the Chair
" Duke of Cleveland.
Lord Tollemache of Helmingham
Lord Egerton of Tatton.

The Minutes of the last Meeting having been read were signed by the Chairman

Lord Egerton reported that all sums due to the Trust had been received with the exception of £5. 16. – in respect of the house

46. Fine penmanship in the Trustees' Minute Book for July 5 1878.

interview with the Police Commissioner, Sir Richard Mayne, and urge constant police supervision. Nor did their fears prove groundless. In June 1890 they asked the Cabmen's Shelter Fund to erect a conspicuous notice warning the cabbies not to enter the garden, and nine years later Lord Derby mentioned the nuisance ('very unpleasant for ladies and children') they were causing – it is not hard to guess the use to which the shrubberies were put.

In short, from about the mid-century onwards the St James's Square Trustees must be regarded as overlords of the garden, and nothing else. Here their main pre-occupations were with whom they should let in, what recreations they should authorize and how the trees, lawns and flower beds should be maintained.

Beyond any doubt, *keys* were the most contentious question. At the heart of it stood the clubs, which obviously had more to gain from access to the garden than most of the semi-absentee residents. The Trustees never felt on firm ground here. The first club to apply for a key was the Windham in 1833. It was turned down, yet the Army & Navy was given one in 1855. Then in 1864 the East India demanded *two* keys, arguing that it paid rates on the equivalent of two houses

(Nos. 16 and 17). This was refused on the excuse of alleged overcrowding, though there were only fourteen actual key-holders at the moment. Nevertheless, for the first and so far as we can trace the only time, the Trustees instructed their Clerk to obtain Counsel's opinion as to their powers. It is frustrating that, if he did so, the result was not put on record. It must have fortified them to some extent, since five years later the East India did not possess even one key and demanded why it was being asked for the sum of £8 19*s* 4*d*, saying that the members 'derived no benefit from the Square'. The committee was curtly told to pay up. On the other hand, when a few years later two short-lived clubs, the Junior Oxford & Cambridge (No. 8) and the Salisbury (No. 12), took the same line – no key no Rate – the Trustees temporized by vainly offering the former a key for the Secretary's use only; in due course both clubs folded, and their arrears were treated as a bad debt.

Keys for dwellers on the periphery of the Square presented rather less of a crux, though it was reported in 1857 that applications were many and were increasing. South-siders (including the Adairs) usually got in on payment of a £2 subscription, and so did the Rectors of St James's and their curates; Dr Bateman of 4 Charles II St maintained a precarious foothold (dislodged in the end), but the Museum of Practical Geology in Jermyn St was turned down flat. Matters of course became much trickier as the character of the Square changed; however, the problem continued to be handled in an empirical manner and was not totally solved even when, in our own time, it was decided to open the garden to all and sundry during most of the working day.

* * *

No doubt because of the comparatively small numbers involved, the nineteenth-century Trustees sometimes showed themselved unexpectedly indulgent to people who wanted to use the garden for something more than fresh air and ambling. Lord Derby and Lord Egerton, the only Trustees present on May 6 1884, must have been in mellow mood when they decided that, as well as admitting perambulators and dogs, 'the game of Lawn Tennis' should be authorized – at that date, of course, it was not much more than a mild and ladylike patball. Then in the mid-1890s the cycling craze hit Society and was allowed to invade the garden. Since the paths were still swoopingly serpentine, it must have been quite fun for the participants but unnerving to the nursemaids and their charges, and soon cycling was forbidden between 10 am and 4 pm. In 1899, however, there was a complaint that Lady Strafford was continuing to charge around at all hours and she had her attention drawn to the rules.

One would like to know just how soon cyclists were debarred from the garden altogether; the tennis-players must have been banished well before 1911, when the Trustees told the Army & Navy Club that it would be 'impossible' to provide tennis courts for the use of the residents.

The garden is such an obviously delightful spot for holding a party that it is a little surprising that nobody seems to have suggested it until 1889, in which year the East India Club (now reconciled with the Trust) asked whether they could use it for 'club entertainments'. The Clerk, in reply,[3] asked for further particulars, but later changed course and said that Trust's Act of Parliament precluded it from allowing any such thing. This sounds like a contrived 'brush-off', and whatever view may be taken of the garden parties and other fiestas of our own time, nobody has ever suggested that they are *ultra vires*.

For a decade after the filling up of the basin in 1855, nothing seems to have been done to improve the appearance and amenities of the garden – in fact they deteriorated to an extent which roused to action the 'ladies of the Square', quiescent since 1818. At the Trustees' June 1864 meeting, the Bishop of Winchester (in the chair) read out the following letter:

> My Lord,
>
> Understanding that a meeting of the Trustees of St James's Square is to be held on the 11th of June, we are desirous of drawing their attention to the very slovenly manner in which the garden is kept, and of submitting to their consideration whether with a little more care it could not be made as pleasant as the other West End squares.
>
> At present the seats are seldom cleaned – the grass irregularly mowed – and dirty paper, dead cats etc are often allowed to remain for days in the bushes.
>
> We suggest that this should be amended and that some flowers planted round the borders might at no great cost add to the cheerfulness of the outlook from the windows, as well as to the pleasure of walking or sitting in the Square, and such additional cost we think would be willingly borne by those who have a right to hold keys.
>
> We would also venture to ask whether the names of the holders of keys of the Square are known to the Trustees and whether these are really restricted to persons entitled to them by the Rules of the Trust.

Commenting some years ago[4] on the signatories to this manifesto, the present writer remarked that 'such formidable characters as Harriett Strafford, Emma Derby, Catherine Tait (wife of the Bishop of London), Anne Hoare and Minnie Tollemache' were buttressed by some male supporters; he should have perceived that 'F. Marlborough', 'C. Cleveland', 'A. F. Cowper', 'M. F. Falmouth' and 'C. E. Egerton of Tatton' were also in fact Duchesses or ladies of lesser title, lightly disguised.

The Bishop was able to assure his colleagues that the gardener, 'acquainted with the above', had promised to bring about an improvement, while Mr Tollemache (No. 10) had volunteered to see it through. The gardener was that same MacArthur who got the contract for extinguishing the basin in 1854, and though his undertaking to the Trustees was followed by some 'hassle' both about his remuneration (£50 per annum) and the effectiveness of his work, it was decided that in view of his long service he should be kept on.

There had been some suggestion of an increase in the Rate to finance the Tollemache reforms, but in the end a voluntary levy of £3 was decided upon for 1865. This brought in £33 from eleven residents (not too good, considering there

47. 2nd Marquess of Londonderry (Lord Castlereagh). By T. Lawrence.

were ten signatories to the ladies' letter alone) and in another whip-round of £2 in the following year, fourteen out of sixteen keyholders paid up. Grumbles over 'untidiness' continued into 1867, when Mr Tollemache was given 'full powers' and presumably exercised them to good effect. He was still active up till 1875 at least; he became Lord Tollemache of Helmingham the following year.

* * *

All through the long Victorian noon-day, the physical appearance of the Square altered hardly at all, except on the West side. There, we have chronicled the rebuilding of No. 14 (London Library) and Nos. 16/17 (East India Club), but there is much of interest also in the fate of Nos. 18 and 19, north and south of the King St corner.

No. 18 was made famous – infamous to some contemporaries – by its association with Robert Stewart, Viscount Castlereagh (2nd Marquess of Londonderry in his final years). We have already seen the mob wreaking its hatred in 1820 (p. 77), but venom pursued the unfortunate statesman after his death by his own hand. Contrary to some tradition he did not actually kill himself at No. 18, but it was there that the distressful symptoms of madness appeared, including, it seems, delusions of homosexual blackmail. On August 11 1822 he went down to his country home at Foots Cray in Kent and the next day, despite his wife's vigilance, managed to get hold of a small penknife and stabbed himself to death.

Princess Lieven[5] records the miserable events of the 20th, when Castlereagh's body, brought back to the Square overnight, was due to be carried in procession to Westminster Abbey. Cobbett, she says, had written 'disgraceful articles', posters were stuck up urging people not to allow a suicide to be buried in the Abbey, and a hostile crowd threatened No. 18. Most of the mourners assembled instead at Westminster – 'a half-measure, a piece of cowardice', the Princess calls it, 'a thing one sees here only too often'.

Let it be recorded, then, that there is much testimony to the charming and civilized hospitality of No. 18. William Rush, the American Envoy,[6] records a magnificent dinner in 1818 where everyone talked French (the British to each other as well as to the foreign guests) and French literature was a principal topic.

After the tragedy of 1822, Castlereagh's widow stayed on at No. 18 until her own death in 1829. The house was then sold for £14,000 to a northern baronet, Sir John Beckett MP, but he never lived there – he and his widow are better known for their long association with Stratford House, Marylebone.[7] No. 18 was let in turn to two clubs – the Oxford & Cambridge (1831–37) and the Army & Navy (1838–45) – both of which were about to move into permanent quarters.

Then came a long lease to the building firm of Elger & Kelk. The redevelopment plans of Sir John Kelk, and their probable effect on No. 17 next door, brought an amazing galaxy of architects to testify for or against – R. C. Carpenter (of Lancing College fame), Sir Charles Barry, Philip Hardwick, (Sir) James Pennethorne and (Sir) William Tite. The alterations which eventually went through also attracted the censure of Dasent, who talks of the 'honest exterior of the house' being 'disfigured by a mask of stucco, according to the ignorant and tasteless fashion of his [Kelk's] day'. This is not quite how most of us would react to what is now Hawker Siddeley House; along with the subsidiary properties in King St which were part of the scheme, it harmonises well enough with the adjacent East India Club.

Dasent, however, has not quite done with No. 18. He goes on to describe it as having been 'degraded to the level of a lodging house', which again seems too severe – the contemporary term 'club chambers' is nearer the mark. One of its tenants, Field-Marshal Lord William Paulet, was actually elected to the St James's Square Trust, but alas there is a pencilled note against the Minute: '*Not eligible – Sir John Kelk still the freeholder*'. This is not strictly accurate, since Kelk was never more than leaseholder under the Becketts and their successors, the Bacons of Lincolnshire. Mr R. E. Balfour, historian of the house,[8] records the variety of uses to which it was put between the remainder of the Kelk lease being bought by an antiques dealer, G. R. Harding, in 1895, and its eventual expiry in 1944.

* * *

We saw in Chapter 1 how the former Capel mansion in St James's Square, on the site of the present No. 19, acquired the name of Cleveland House when Charles Fitzroy, King Charles II's son by Barbara Villiers, Duchess of Cleveland, took up residence there in 1721.[9]

The Fitzroy male line failed in 1774 and Cleveland House passed to the 2nd Duke's nephew, Henry Vane, 3rd Earl of Darlington, who was in due course created Marquess and then Duke of Cleveland. The editor of *The Complete Peerage* is magnificently scathing about this transaction:

> It is a cause for wonder (he says) that the head of the historic house of Vane of Raby should have so prided himself on a bastard descent from an infamous adulteress that when he obtained a step in the peerage, he changed his title to that of *Cleveland*, a peerage conferred on his notorious ancestress as the actual wage of her sin – one, too, which had not been redeemed from the slur on it by any merit of her successors, one of whom was a fool and the other a nonentity.[10]

The situation was hardly improved by the new Duke's second marriage to a certain Elizabeth Russell, daughter of a market gardener and reputed former mistress of old Coutts the banker. Creevey[11] is almost as rude about her as *The Complete Peerage* is about her husband – 'a brazen-faced pop' he cheerfully calls her, and marvels that the Duke should have placed her over his daughters.

Nevertheless the second Cleveland dynasty, fortified by immense wealth (property in every English county, so 'twas said), established itself for a full century in the great, foursquare old mansion, almost unchanged since Richard Frith sold it to Lord Essex in the 1670s. It was in 1891 that the line petered out once more, with the death of the third of three brothers to hold the title. This 4th Duke is described as a splendidly picturesque old man, tall and erect, receiving his guests in his star and ribbon of the Garter. Catherine, his Duchess (previously married to Lord Dalmeny), was certainly a character! She spent much of her time at Battle Abbey in Sussex, where she edited the so-called *Battle Roll* and was a familiar sight riding about the little town on her donkey. In London, she naturally preferred a grander steed; we probably owe to James Cox, the London Library's famous Assistant Librarian (1882–1952), the enchanting legend of the Duchess, at the age of 70, riding up on a coal-black charger to

48. No. 19 (Old Cleveland House). Demolished c. *1892.*

change her books, an open umbrella held aloft.[12]

Soon after the last Duke's death, Cleveland House was sold for demolition, surprisingly unlamented by Dasent. He declares that for many years before, its appearance had been more curious than pleasing, in spite of some handsome chimneypieces, gilded ceilings and polished floors. 'Such relics of London,' he continues, 'are foredoomed to destruction as soon as their owners fail to keep them in reasonable repair'; in the case of Cleveland House the value of the site was too great to permit the retention of such a 'mouldering vestige of antiquity'. There is a painfully familiar ring about this argument!

But Dasent was right on values. A certain Mr Gabriel paid £50,000 for the 'mouldering vestige' and when he pulled it down it was found to have walls three or four feet thick and 'bonding timbers of English oak, as sound as when they were placed in position more than two hundred years ago'.

The subsequent fate of this site is unique in St James's Square, in that the successor building, a florid and turreted affair by Messrs Rolfe & Matthews, has itself been demolished and replaced by a third Cleveland House in a strictly 'contemporary' style (p. 151).

The disappearance of the first one in 1894 was about the final historical event recorded by Arthur Dasent, whose *History*, so precious to every later chronicler, was published by Macmillan only a year later. He seems to have continued his topographical researches, rounding them off with Grosvenor Square in 1935. In the Civil Service, his career covered an even greater span, in fact it has been described as straddling 'two worlds as well as two centuries';[13] beginning as a junior in the Duchy of Lancaster Office in 1879, when Gladstone's Home Rule campaign was in full flood, he finished up as Clerk to the Parliament of Northern Ireland.

XIII
Towards the Brink

As they approached the twentieth century, the inhabitants of St James's Square can have had little inkling of the two destructive forces lying in wait for them – war on a global scale, and explosives not only as an international but a domestic instrument of terror.

Yet as early as 1884, three years in advance of Queen Victoria's Jubilee, the Square had caught an unnerving glimpse of what was to come. For Londoners of that day, the Fenian Brotherhood had much the same sinister connotation as its modern successor, the IRA. Its campaigns[1] followed the only too familiar formula of devices, usually cakes or sticks of dynamite, planted in public locations. As a rule few people were hurt, though the damage to property could be considerable. After some escalation the previous year, 1884 opened with a plan of attack against several London termini; only at Victoria did a bomb actually go off, causing great destruction. Then, at about 9 o'clock on the night of May 31, the West End was shaken by three explosions. One turned out to be in a lavatory just opposite New Scotland Yard, the other two in St James's Square. The latter had been carefully planned, but not quite carefully enough. Both targets were offshoots of the War Office – Adair House at the western end of the South side, headquarters of the Intelligence Branch; and No. 21, where various sections had been housed since the Bishops of Winchester moved out in 1875. Currently, the Military Education Branch was in possession.

However the conspirators side-slipped. The device intended for Adair House was actually placed in the basement entrance to the Junior Carlton Club kitchen next door; that aimed at No. 21 was apparently lowered by a string onto a ledge a few feet below Sir Watkin Williams Wynn's dining-room window at No. 20. In each case 'bags of dynamite' (believed to be of American origin) were set off by fuses instead of the clockwork mechanism favoured up till then.

The Junior Carlton explosion was the more spectacular. Though nobody was killed, several women in the busy club kitchen received cuts and bruises – the chef, in the direct line of fire, only had his tall cap blown off. At No. 20, the housekeeper was in the front basement room with the shutters open, but in spite of the windows (back as well as front) being shattered, she and the rest of the staff were unhurt.

First on the spot was Police Sergeant Bitten, who had just been giving orders to a man 'specially posted for the protection of a nobleman in the neighbourhood' (whom may that have been, one wonders). He found the Square plunged in darkness by the fracturing of a gas main; terrified horses from the South side cab-rank were bolting in all directions (the controversial Shelter just opposite the Junior Carlton was undamaged); windows had been broken and pictures sometimes sent crashing to the ground as far away as Cleveland House.

We today can only too easily imagine the sequel, with the Square cordoned off and police reinforcements pouring in from all over the Metropolitan area. By then of course the dynamiters (believed to have been a gang of three) had escaped and were never brought to justice. It was Whitsun Bank Holiday weekend, and the next morning (Saturday), quite apart from coveys of peers and peeresses, and even members of the Royal Family, flocking into the Junior Carlton kitchen, the goggling crowds were able to repeat their sight-seeing of the previous Easter, when the Local Government Office in Whitehall was attacked. But our own thoughts go forward inevitably to the tragic events at the diagonally opposite corner of the Square in April 1984.

* * *

Fenianism died down, and no further alarms disturbed the placid surface of St James's Square life during the old Queen's last days or beneath the indulgent eye of her eldest son. But that does not mean that nothing had changed. For example, that War Office occupancy of No. 21 is a reminder that though we have noted the incursion of *embassies*, *businesses* and *clubs*, there has been but slight reference so far to *government departments*. The first to get a brief foothold, long ago, was the Board of Admiralty (No. 13, 1723–25) – just a decanting operation while its premises in Whitehall were being rebuilt. The Charity Commissioners were at No. 8 from 1855 to 1876, but the longest occupancy by a single department up to the present day began in 1852, when the Copyhold, Inclosure and Tithe Commission rented No. 3 from the Duke of Leeds; the Commission, and its successors the Board and then the Ministry of Agriculture, were to remain there until 1922. It is perhaps a little surprising that the Square did not attract more learned societies or professional bodies – the only instances one can trace before World War I are that for a time, according to Dasent, the Statistical and

49. The St James's Square basement of the Junior Carlton Club, after the Fenian outrage of 31 May 1884.

Philological Societies and the Institute of Actuaries shared No. 14 with the London Library.

At least one house lost, and then regained, its traditional function. From the moment in 1770 when No. 32 was bought from Lord Warwick as a town house for Richard Terrick, 100th Bishop of London, and his successors, remarkably little is heard from them in the context of the Square. The very names of the next three – Lowth, Beilby Porteous, Randolph – awake hardly an echo. As we have seen, Bishop Howley (1814–28) left a physical mark by having No. 32 rebuilt, and his successor, Blomfield, served the Trust quite conscientiously. But under none of them did London House, as it was usually called, compare with the social and ecclesiastical powerhouse which No. 21 became during the long reign of Sumner of Winchester. Things brightened up a bit with the arrival of Archibald Tait (1857). Successor to Arnold at Rugby, he had never held a see when he took over London House. He was certainly a missionary bishop, prepared to preach anywhere – 'omnibus yards, ragged schools, Covent Garden market, gypsy encampments' – and he was well backed up by his forceful wife Catherine.

After the Taits' inevitable translation to Canterbury in 1868, the Bishops of London seem to have retreated almost entirely to Fulham Palace. Dasent describes No. 32 as empty and silent at the time he was writing, 'save on those rare occasions when it is galvanised into temporary usefulness for the purposes of a charity bazaar or a missionary meeting.'

It was Mandell Creighton, when he succeeded the famous William Temple in 1897, who brought the old house back to life. By then, it was in a 'deplorable condition' and the Diocesan Architect, W. D. Caroe, had to renovate it from top to toe, with due attention to the drains, no less than to the room which was to be used as a chapel. When at length she moved in, Mrs Creighton felt 'more in the world' than at Fulham – 'but oh how much of the world there is! The flesh and the devil are not nearly so dangerous combined.'[2]

In the end the Creightons enjoyed only a brief tenure at No. 32, the Bishop dying in the year 1900. However, his successor, that somewhat flamboyant public figure Dr Arthur Winnington-Ingram made vigorous use of the house. He had been worried and even conscience-stricken at first when, as a bachelor of 41, he found himself inheriting a suburban palace with thirty-two bedrooms and a town mansion with seventeen, but his evangelical zeal and wide human sympathies soon filled both with all-embracing hospitality.[3] After a year, the Bishop took the unorthodox step of publishing a 'Statement of Account', itemizing everything from 'Hire of four horses in constant use, £210' (plus £326 5*s* 0*d* for 'forage, shoeing and tooling') to 'St James's Square Trust, £4 13*s* 0*d*', and showing that he had had to spend £700 over his official salary of £10,000.

Winnington-Ingram managed to keep London House, as well as Fulham, afloat until 1921, when the Caledonian Club took a lease of No. 32 with an option (exercised in 1939) to buy at the next vacancy of the See.

Otherwise, private ownership remained the general rule. At No. 33, next door to London House, continuity was demonstrated by the 14th, 15th and 16th Earls of Derby, after the 14th's move there from No. 10 in 1854; it was the 17th Earl (brother of his predecessor) who sold 'Derby House' to the English & Scottish Law Life Assurance in 1912, whereby it became enmeshed in the Square's next wave of commercial development. Society still flocked to No. 4, to enjoy the

50. Arthur Winnington-Ingram, Bishop of London (1900–39). By Frank Salisbury.

hospitality and admire the magnificent pictures of the Cowper family.[4] At No. 5, the Byng identification with the Square, so marked in the days of George Byng MP (and not just in the matter of carpet-beating!), was intensified once more when, not long after the death in a railway accident of the 4th Earl of Strafford (1899), his nephew – then known as Lord Enfield, but later the 6th Earl – established himself as a dominant Trustee and remained so for the next quarter of a century. And so things went on, with a few exceptions, all round the Square. Its solemn entertainments seldom made the headlines – it was fortuitous that Kaiser William II was received at Norfolk House almost on the eve of World War I, or that his mighty antagonist Lord Kitchener dined there the night before his fatal embarkation in HMS *Hampshire* on June 5 1916.

Among the private owners, there was some interesting new blood. One landmark was the purchase of No. 11 by the Hon. Rupert Guinness (later 2nd Earl of Iveagh) in 1906. After Robert Adam's refurbishment for Sir Rowland Winn (p. 43), this house proved a magnet to the rich – some of them the 'new rich' – of their day. They included two members of the Hoare family of bankers,[5] Sir Richard, 2nd bart. in 1787–88, and his distant cousin, Henry Hoare of Iden, in 1865–75. In between came, among others, the dubious financier Alexander Davison and Hudson Gurney, of the great Norfolk merchant tribe.

A fascinating character, this Hudson. Disowned by the Society of Friends after he subscribed to a Defence Fund during the Napoleonic Wars, he blossomed out into pink shirts and ornamental boots, and when he bought No. 11 in 1823 made it the scene of tireless entertaining – '76 dinner parties and a ball in 160 days', as he unconvincingly complained. Election as MP for Newtown in the Isle of Wight in no way cramped his style, since he made it a condition that he would never have to set foot in the place. Yet like every Gurney, he had a serious side, witness his fellowship of the Royal Society and other learned bodies and his aspiration to write 'just one good poem'.[6]

When Hudson died, aged 90, in 1864, he left No. 11 (along with over a million pounds made out of banking and brewing) to his cousin and nephew-in-law, John Henry Gurney, who either let or sold it to Henry Hoare aforesaid. It then passed successively through the hands of two more millionaire MPs, Sir Joseph Bailey and Mr J. M. McCalmont, and it was the latter who sold out to the Hon. Rupert Guinness in 1906. Mr Guinness was immediately appointed a Trustee, and thus established a family link with the administration of the Square which was not broken until 1979.

Three years after the Guinness incursion came something more dramatic – the creation of what was virtually a brand-new, full-size residence in St James's Square. Since about 1897 three bachelor brothers called Farrer had occupied No. 23, on the South side, but following the death of Earl Egerton (formerly Lord Egerton of Tatton) in 1909, they acquired No. 7. Two of the brothers, William and Henry, were solicitors (partners in the still eminent firm of Farrer & Co.), while the third, Gaspard, was a merchant banker (Baring Bros.). What they wanted was a house where they could have their individual suites but could share the entertaining-rooms, notably a dining-room and an immense library. Edwin Lutyens was already working on their Kentish mansion, the Salutation at Sandwich; he was now invited to demolish No. 7 (save perhaps for some outer walls) and rebuild it to the brothers' specification. By 1911 they were able to move in.

51. Gaspard Farrer, who managed and financed the garden for twenty years.

When the present writer first took note of No. 7, perhaps twenty years ago, it was Ministry of Labour offices, and that is exactly what it looks like – nothing remotely domestic about the prim rows of windows without reveals and the formal Ionic porch; only the almost invisible roof-line and chimneys mitigate what Alastair Service calls 'a frontage of extraordinarily flat relief'.[7] Inside, the formidable oak staircase and the entertaining-rooms aforesaid, with their neo-Carolean columns and pilasters and great carved swags of fruit and flowers give an effect of gloomy grandeur; excellent mid-term Lutyens stuff in their way, but as a London lodgement for three bachelors – mind-boggling! No. 7 had elaborate staff and stabling arrangements at the back which included a coachman's (or chauffeur's) flat. The Farrers did not need this, and in about 1912 lent it to Lutyens as an office where he could work on his *magnum opus*, Viceroy's House, New Delhi. As Sir Edwin's biographer remarks, 'there was a delightful incongruity in designing a palace in a coachman's bedroom, the address of which was 7 Apple Tree Yard'. For some time, incidentally, he had as neighbour the painter, Sir William Nicholson, whose leasing of No. 11 from Lord Strafford led to the 'conversation piece' reproduced on p. 146. No more cosy roosts for artists or architects in Apple Tree Yard today – nothing but offices on one side and Jermyn St dustbins on the other.[8]

However, the Farrer brothers, especially Gaspard, were to mean much more to the Square than even their creation of a new No. 7. The story starts in about 1909–10, when the garden was sadly overgrown and when the statue of King William was, according to Lord Edward Gleichen,[9] 'rediscovered' by Sir

Schomberg MacDonnell of the Office of Works – as though he had had to hack his way in with a machete . . . Sir Schomberg reported not only that the obstructing trees ought to be cleared, but that the statue itself was in a deplorable condition – filthy and with serious flaws in the metalwork, in fact in danger of falling. In December 1910 the Treasury agreed that the Commissioners of Works should take it over and repair it at a cost not exceeding £125.

Technically, this could only be done (under the Public Statues (Metropolis) Act of 1854) with the agreement of the owners. But who were the owners? Nobody knew. The Trustees had merely 'consented' to the statue's erection by Samuel Travers' residual legatees (p. 35). Eventually, Mr Seccombe, of Works, had a meeting with Lord Enfield and Lord Kinnaird, as a result of which the Trustees undertook to 'assume' ownership and immediately carry out the transfer. The quaint transaction went through, and some time during 1911 the statue was removed to the workshops of Messrs A. B. Burton at Thames Ditton for a thorough overhaul. Among other things, it was discovered that King William's cloak and the horse's tail needed extensive first-aid and that one of the hind legs would actually have to be replaced.

Coupled with the Office of Works' offer to take over the statue was a 'requirement' that the Trustees should in future keep the garden in better order and attractively bedded out; more significantly, its layout should be altered so that King William could be viewed from 'the various roads converging on the Square'.

These ideas were reinforced by a communication from Colonel Willis, of the Windham Club, Col. Owen of the Army & Navy and Major Talbot of the Sports – the first appearance of the clubs in a constructive rôle – urging that the garden should be made more beautiful and attractive, especially in Coronation year. Accordingly the Clerk was instructed to get in touch with the Director of Kew Gardens, who in turn put him on to a Mr W. Goldring, of Kew Gardens Rd. Mr Goldring's ideas for 'broad avenues to the statue and other improvements', were accepted at a Trustees' meeting on January 5 1912, and Mr Guinness undertook to obtain estimates, at his own expense, for carrying out the work. At a further meeting on April 18 the estimate (unspecified) of Messrs James Carter, the famous seedsman, was accepted and at Mr Guinness' suggestion a Mr Roberts Wray was invited to 'overlook' the job, for which, it appears, he had actually prepared the plans.

All this seems straightforward, but it conflicts strangely with the widespread notion that the alterations to the garden were planned by Sir Edwin Lutyens, paid for by Mr Gaspard Farrer and not executed until after World War I. The Lutyens element in the story is complicated by the fact that in writing to his wife on September 12 1912, he mentions 'a letter from Mrs Astor's secretary, asking me to do a garden in St James's Square'.[10] It was in the previous year that Waldorf Astor and his subsequently famous wife had taken over No. 4, and Astor himself had been elected a Trustee. But neither the Astor nor the Lutyens

52. No. 7, the Staircase. Sir Edwin Lutyens (1910–11).

archives throw any further light on this démarche, and we simply do not know whether it related to the Square itself or to the miniature garden, or courtyard, still to be found behind No. 4 – Lutyens did sometimes oblige with little schemes of this kind for his friends.

The whole subject then sinks out of sight (there were other things to think about between 1914 and 1918), breaking surface again – or seeming to do so – with a Trustees' minute of May 12 1921:

53. Sir Edwin Lutyens, O.M. By Robert Lutyens.

> Agreed that no further steps be taken with reference to the repair and painting of the railings until Sir Edwin Lutyens' report, which is being obtained by Mr Farrer, is presented and considered.

Unfortunately, this report is something else which has vanished, but a year later (May 24 1922) the Trustees were informed that

> Mr Gaspard Farrer . . . had carried out at his own expense extensive alterations and improvements to the garden and had intimated his intention to personally bear the expense of upkeep for the present.

'The present' actually extended itself to the year 1941, during the whole of which time Gaspard Farrer took the garden into his care, choosing the trees and plants

54. 'Washington Inn' erected in the garden during World War I.

and paying both for them and for day-to-day upkeep – an act of unmatched generosity.

As for those initial 'alterations and improvements' of his, even if as now seems likely, they did *not* include the basic layout of the paths, there must have been plenty which needed setting to rights in St James's Square. Though the direct impact of World War I on the civilian life of London was incomparably less than that of its terrible successor, there were for example Zeppelin and bomber plane raids which came sufficiently close for some St James's Square folk to take improvised precautions. And so it happened that on the night of March 3 1918 Mrs Guinness descended to the dining-room of No. 11 for the birth of her second daughter, still happily with us as Patricia, Lady Boyd of Merton. Just as well, the family must have thought, when, only four nights later, a savage raid killed twenty-three people and injured some forty in the St John's Wood and Paddington area.

Physically, the Square garden suffered its first and so far last intrusion of the builders' men. At a special meeting on October 9 1917 the Trustees had before them an application by the War Works Council of the American YMCA to be allowed to erect an Officers' Hostel within the sacred enclosure. Backed as it was by the General Officer Commanding, London District (General Sir Francis Lloyd), the request was immediately granted, and there arose in the southern reaches of the garden the substantial structure which can be glimpsed in the illustration opposite. The only conditions imposed were that gas or electricity should be used for heating and cooking, rather than solid fuel (a thought for the trees, no doubt) and that the 'Y' should pay for ultimate reinstatement.

'Washington Inn', as it came to be called, was rather a latecomer in the time-scale of World War I; nevertheless on November 8 1918, only three days before the Armistice, the Trustees agreed to the buildings being extended – preferably without a proposed billiard-room. In the end these works were not carried out, but the pressure on accommodation in London for young officers continued to be such that the lease was prolonged until the end of 1920.

All this, and the comings and goings of men in khaki – plus no doubt the wounded soldiers in their 'blues', invited into the garden from Lady Ridley's Hospital in Carlton House Terrace and from Charing Cross – was observed and remembered by a sharp-eyed young lady at No. 20. Her father, the Earl of Strathmore & Kinghorne, had taken a lease[11] of the house from the Williams Wynns the year after the Guinness family came to No. 11 and had been elected a Trustee on March 26 1908. Earlier, Lord and Lady Strathmore and their children had rather 'pigged it' in a flat in Grosvenor Gardens, and No. 20 was the result of an exciting house-hunting expedition. We shall have more to say in subsequent chapters about the association with the Square of Lady Elizabeth Bowes-Lyon, now HM Queen Elizabeth the Queen Mother.

XIV

Butlers, Bombs and Ernest Bevin

St James's Square 'between the Wars' remained on the whole very much as Arnold Bennett described it in 1918 – 'the cardiac region of St James's, the Square itself, where knights, baronets, barons, brewers, viscounts, marquesses, hereditary marshals and chief butlers, dukes, bishops, banks, librarians and Government departments gaze during the four seasons at the statue of a Dutchman'.[1] Of course the 'carriage folk' were thinning out, but the amount of space we have had to give to architectural and occupational changes ought not to obscure the fact that in the first forty or so years of the twentieth century, no less than in the eighteenth and nineteenth, the Square continued to a fair degree as a place of gaiety and grandeur. Even the new generation of owners moved in with panache. When Rupert and Gwendolen Guinness were presented with the freehold of No. 11 by the former's father, they built a complete new floor of servants' rooms on the roof and then gave a terrific housewarming ball:

> Wearing a pale blue velvet gown wrought with silver thread, a tiara of diamonds tipped with pear-shaped pearls and a high pearl collar, Gwendolen stood at the head of the staircase, which was smothered with crimson and pink rambler roses, pink peonies and trails of smilax, and greeted her guests, a vast array of the nobility.[2]

The arrival of the Strathmores at No. 20 was the signal for assemblies of a more heavyweight kind, with imperial overtones; there is a record of four ex-Viceroys – Lansdowne, Elgin, Curzon and Minto – round the dinner table on the same evening. Though as time went on the little Lady Elizabeth graduated from a nursery at the back of the second floor to a schoolroom lower down (p. 158), her rôle in most of these entertainments was limited to hanging over the banisters to watch the glamorous arrivals and listen to the hired orchestra in full blow. Meanwhile her own routine moved on from childish games round the statue of King William with her brother David (p. 139) to dancing classes shared with a little circle of beloved friends. The future Queen was only 21 when the Strathmore lease of No. 20 came to an end in 1921 but, as we shall see, she has still not lost her memories of that happy interlude of youth.

At No. 4 the Astors effortlessly absorbed the rituals of their adopted country – Mr Lee, their famous butler, saw to it that the footmen wore powder whenever there were eight or more guests to dinner. One such occasion was no doubt in 1917, when there was a grand party in honour of Mr Lloyd George's 56th birthday. There was only one candle on the cake, however, to symbolize the first year of his Premiership, and every guest had to cut a slice without disturbing it – omen for a long and prosperous reign!

Mention of footmen reminds us that the staffing of the great London houses, at any rate during the season, remained at a high and remarkably uniform level throughout the whole history of St James's Square as a residential quarter. In the late seventeenth century, Ormonde House was looked after by some forty-five household servants, exclusive of stable staff; the Norfolk House return of *Daily Numbers . . . for whom a Table is Provided* (1857–61)[3] showed twenty-two servants in the servants' hall, seven in the steward's room, four in the kitchen and five in the nursery – total (indoors) thirty-eight; while Mr Sykes declares that the records of Northumberland, Bedford, Devonshire and Shelborne Houses indicate that forty was about the average, and so continued right up to 1914.[4] '*Except on party nights, what on earth did they do with themselves?*', is one's inevitable reaction to-day. Even the most modest St James's Square establishments would have been considered under-staffed on less than nine or ten domestics, divided more or less equally between kitchen, housemaids and hall, with valets and lady's maids in addition.

Backstage, so to speak, matters no doubt remained fairly primitive. Someone who knew a couple of the old Howard servants in their retirement, used to hear how they dreaded the annual migration from Arundel to St James's Square for 'the season'; the kitchen, they declared, was 'in the next street'[5] and it was virtually impossible to serve meals hot. Moreover, such journeys were not just once-a-year affairs; on the contrary we are assured that during the 1920s and '30s, butler, cook and the entire staff commuted regularly between the Castle and Norfolk House in an enormous 'Black Maria'.[6]

Of course, World War I made fearful and permanent inroads into the ranks of the St James's Square menservants, but a diminished posse of them was soon ornamenting its front halls once more, and no doubt sharing in the general bedazzlement with the antics of the 'bright young people' of the 1920s. These seem to have engulfed the staidest as well as the most dashing West End mansions. Quite apart from a notorious episode in 1928, when Lady Ellesmere threw a gang of semi-aristocratic gate-crashers out of Bridgewater House, St James's, it is a little unexpected to read of Norfolk House as the final goal of an all-night 'treasure hunt', with a splendid breakfast to greet the hunters and 'a string band to cheer them after their strenuous adventures'.[7]

* * *

The continued vitality of the 'private sector' did not disguise the fact that the Trustees could hardly hope to look to it indefinitely for recruitment. By 1924, they were down to only seven, and at the May 22 meeting, with the Earl of Strafford, as usual, in the chair, it was decided to invite Mr (later Sir Charles) Hagberg Wright, of the London Library (No. 14), Mr A. D. Besant of the Clerical, Medical & General Life Assurance Society (No. 15) and Mr G. White of the East India Club (No. 16) to become Trustees; the successors to these three neighbours have continued to serve and support the Trust until the present day.

It may be noted that the *eligibility* of such corporate bodies, or their officers, was not apparently called into question at the time, though it has been occasionally since. For example, some unease about the legal position was clearly present at the November 1957 meeting when, with numbers again inadequate, seven gentlemen (all, with the exception of Mr McRobert of the Arts Council, Secretaries or Managers of commercial firms) were sent invitations to join 'in their personal capacity'. This of course was just what they were not entitled to do; at best they could be classified with the 'Landlords, Owners or Proprietors' who under Clause V of the 1726 Act had to pay rates on houses occupied by foreign Ambassadors.

It happens that the whole question of the ownership and management of the London squares was thoroughly explored between the Wars. In August 1927 a Warrant was issued to 'Our Trusty and Entirely Beloved Cousin and Counsellor Charles Stewart, Marquess of Londonderry' for a Royal Commission which, under his Chairmanship, was to enquire and report on

> Squares and similar open spaces in the area of the Administrative County of London, with special reference to the conditions on which they are held and used and the desirability of their preservation as open spaces, and to recommend whether any or all of them shall be permanently safeguarded . . . and if so under what terms and conditions.

The Royal Commission presented its Report[8] to Parliament in September 1928 – good going, considering that the members had to pass in review some 461 gardens or similar enclosures, of which 63 (including of course St James's Square) were controlled by special Acts of Parliament and no fewer than 223 were still in private ownership, subject only to any rights of user granted to residents. Every enclosure appears to have been inspected by groups of commissioners in person and is individually described. This is what they said about St James's Square:

55. Lady Elizabeth Bowes-Lyon (now Queen Elizabeth the Queen Mother) with her brother David, a fancy-dress photograph of 1909.

> Laid out about the year 1663 [*correct for the Square, certainly not for the garden*]. An enclosure square in shape, very attractively laid out as a lawn with some fine trees. The privet hedge and shrubs around the border have been removed in parts, admitting to a view across the open space from outside. Overlooked by large dwelling-houses, clubs and offices.

The Commission's most significant recommendations were that while it was important that all but five of the gardens should be permanently preserved, Local Authorities should not be given compulsory powers of acquisition except in cases of neglect (para. 58); on the other hand the *owner* of an enclosure, with the consent of 75 per cent of the persons – if any – entitled to 'use and enjoyment', should be empowered to *require* the London County Council to take it over and vest it in the relevant Borough Council as a public open space (para. 94). All this was to become highly relevant to our story some forty years later.

Legalities apart, the commissioners had interesting thoughts about Square gardens as such. They pleaded for the replacement of thick, heavy iron railings with something more civilized and for the removal, at least in part, of privet hedges and/or shrubberies round the perimeters, 'giving an untidy appearance, particularly in winter, and completely obscuring the view of the delightful lawns and flowers', not only from the public but from the ground-floor windows of the facing houses. What is more, the Report goes on specifically to praise the 'contrivance of wide openings in the existing hedges', which now provided an uninterrupted view across St James's Square' (paras. 95–8).

A special accolade, then, for the latter, but only confirming what a contributor to *The Times* had had to say about 'St James's Lawns', as he calls them, a few years before.[9] All winter, he recalls, he had been blundering about with some Mediterranean scene in his mind's eye, but now, suddenly and belatedly, he has 'discovered' the Square, complete with King William III's statue and his great horse, 'of the true Flemish breed'. Henceforward, when he groped his way in November to the 'bookish cosiness' of the London Library, he would remember the 'Lawns' as they were that spring, and take heart.

It is notable that this writer, recollecting how for the 'duration', the place was all huts and typewriters and mess, praises the Authorities, who had not been content merely to restore what was there before, but had provided a much better version. In 1913, he declares, St James's Square was 'a thicket of grimy shrubs' which you couldn't see across. Now, ancient openness had returned, while keeping the amenity of a garden; big trees had been cut down, shrubberies uprooted, wide lawns laid out, magnolias and other flowering things ringed the circuit – 'space, light, grateful shadow, gentle grandeur . . .'

A clear impression here that the Square's emergence from the 'grimy shrubs' era was a post-War phenomenon, and it may well be that while the new layout of the paths had been achieved before August 1914, the more detailed improvements were due to the inspiration as well as the generosity of Gaspard Farrer. It is certain that in 1924 and 1925 respectively the Trust received from him sizeable refunds of £187 and £161 for money it had spent on the Garden after he had undertaken to bear the whole cost (p. 134), and finally it was arranged that he should deal with 'Mr Rassell' direct. For a first reference in Trust Minutes to the still flourishing firm of Rassell & Co., nurserymen of Earls Court Rd, we have to go back to May 1913, when a maintenance contract at £76 per annum was signed with them, 'Hyde the gardener' having resigned. The connection was renewed after the War and proved remarkably durable, but at last in 1939 Mr Farrer reported that he was now employing Messrs James Comber, who had taken over Rassells' long-time gardener.

Meanwhile, at one AGM after another, the Trustees recorded their appreciation of the 'beautiful way' the garden was being maintained and of Mr Farrer's bounty, and this only ceased in the year 1941, when all but utilitarian gardening (colour plate III) had to be suspended under the imperatives of World War II.

* * *

On possible public access to Square gardens, the 1927 Commissioners took on the whole a conservative line, suggesting only (para. 59) that the admission of children, 'under suitable arrangements for supervision and control', ought not to have any seriously adverse effect on property, and advocating quite strongly that Local Authorities should try to secure this. Yet they also hinted at something much more revolutionary for the future, when they drew attention (para. 98) to the existence in various parts of London of 'grass plots without railings, or protected only with posts and chains'; such arrangements, they thought, might well be given an extended trial and could help to form a healthy public opinion on the subject. A clear pointer towards the state of affairs now existing in Grosvenor, Hanover, and many another square!

However, the St James's Square Trustees took a cautious step forward on their own. At the May 1933 meeting they agreed unanimously that the gates of the garden should be left open every week-day in August between 12.30 pm and 2.30 pm; the gardener to report any damage to the Clerk, who would be empowered to withdraw the privilege at his discretion. No vandalism resulted, it would seem, since the concession was repeated the following year, and in 1935 was extended to cover September as well – only provided that the gate opposite Charles II St was kept closed, to avoid the garden being used as a 'short cut through to St James's St'.

While the Trustees were already aware that their writ no longer ran beyond the perimeter of the garden, they were fully alert to any threat to the latter, whether from outside or even from below. It is slightly surprising to find the Royal Commission already confronted in 1927 with the concept of *underground car parks* in the squares (para. 69). Some of the landowners had urged, through their *ad hoc* Committee, that they should be allowed to deal with the subsoil in this or any other way they thought fit, so long as it did not interfere with the surface as an open space. The Commissioners acquiesced, subject to schemes being approved by the LCC.

The Trustees of St James's Square thought differently, and at least three times since have taken a firm stand. The first occasion was in May 1935, when a certain Mr Drummond Bone and Mr Gordon Glover put forward plans for a 'rotary garage' beneath the Square, powers for which could be taken under the 'Restriction of Ribbon Development Bill (Clause II)', then before Parliament. The Trustees' rejection was unanimous, and they instructed their Clerks to monitor any moves by Westminster City Council.

No more was heard of this or any other proposal until March 24 1953, when the Trustees had good reason to believe that their garden was seriously at risk. This was because a Working Party[10] appointed by the then Minister of Transport had not only come out in favour of underground garages in the London squares, but had chosen St James's Square as its 'guinea pig'. There were a mere seven illustrations in its Report, but all related to the Square: engravings (States 1 & 2 of Sutton Nicholls), chosen to buttress the Working Party's contention that such areas were originally open and treeless; three photographs of a model showing the proposed garage and its approaches, and the new layout of the garden; and two 'artist's impressions'. One of the latter was for a garage with the 'greatest possible capacity' (700 cars), which would involve removing all the trees, and the other a smaller scheme (420 cars), preserving a few of them. In each case King William's statue was to be shunted to the West side of the Square and given a setting of seats and flower-beds.

In spite of formidable new features such as 'staircase partitions, ventilation towers and ramps', it was argued by the 'eminent architects' (Messrs Wornum and Playne) that they were providing a feeling of repose, opening the Square to the enjoyment of all and enhancing the 'strong architectural character' of the buildings themselves.

It is a relief to turn to p. 22 of the Report, where a Reservation by Mr C. D. (later Sir Colin) Buchanan blows these extraordinary propositions sky-high. They would destroy, he believed, something which he and a great many other people had come to value possibly more than any other feature of Central London – compared with the 'magnificence' of the trees, the St James's Square model revealed a poor scene. Moreover, such clearance, far from enhancing the effect of the buildings, would in many cases merely emphasize the loss of their original character.

The Trustees, for their part, expressed astonishment that the amenities of the 'earliest and most famous London Square' should be threatened in this way. Active opposition was promised and a propaganda campaign discussed, but once again the danger evaporated, and in fact only a handful of garages have ever been excavated below the open spaces of Central London.

Nevertheless, in May 1962, there was one last approach, this time by the firm of Alexander Geddes Ltd. The reaction was predictable – 'inform them', the

56. Artist's impression of the proposed underground car-parking scheme (1953), looking towards the north-west corner, with most of the garden trees destroyed.

Trustees directed their Clerk, 'that we are not interested in such a development'.

Parking *above* ground proved a menace not so easily disposed of. Unease on the subject had been first expressed as far back as 1914. What worried the Trustees particularly was the 'great damage' which they believed the petrol fumes were doing to the trees and shrubs, and though they do not seem to have been successful in getting chapter and verse for this from Messrs Rassell or other experts, they urged time and again between the Wars that at least cars should be compulsorily parked with their engines facing the Square rather than the garden. The 'authorities' turned a deaf ear, nor did the Trustees do any better with a plea that part of the parking space should be reserved for the clubs. 'Clockwise traffic' in the Square dates from 1935, only some 24 years after Mrs Astor was complaining that the corner location of her new home at No. 4 made *such* difficulties for the horses on the night of a party.

* * *

If one had only the Minutes of the Trust to go by, the immediate impact of World War II upon St James's Square was not exactly dramatic. However, the Trustees did convene specially on December 9 1939 to consider a request from Westminster City Council for their concurrence in the erection of air raid shelters to accommodate 500 persons. Only three Trustees turned up, but Mr Gaspard Farrer (in the chair) said he had been in touch with the Earl of Strafford on the subject. His Lordship's advice was that while he did not believe they could stop the Council from building shelters if it was determined to, he nevertheless counselled resistance. So a letter was sent which thanked the Council for its 'courteous' request, but continued:

> They [the Trustees] would point out that nearly every house in the Square affords area or other protection to the public, many of them sandbagged, etc. – that from midnight to 10 a.m. the Square is practically deserted, and that in the most populous hours of the day there are never 500 people in it, or its immediate vicinity – or anything like that number.

In the circumstances the Trustees regretted the public expenditure involved, hoped the scheme would be abandoned and asked that their letter should be put before the Minister for Home Security.

Well argued, perhaps, but rather too much in the spirit of the 'phoney' war? No reply is recorded[11] and it is somewhat remarkable that the Minutes of the next AGM (May 22 1940) make no reference to the war whatsoever. Not until April 1941 is there mention of the Square being 'used' by Westminster City Council and other authorities, in consequence of which no Rate would be levied to 'keep the Square tidy'.

This provided an answer for the Marquess of Bristol (No. 6); he had asked whether the Rate need be paid on premises made uninhabitable by enemy action, which by then had caused untidiness in the Square on an alarming scale. By far the worst incident was on the evening of October 14 1940, when the premises of the Canada Life Assurance Co. at No. 2 were completely demolished by a direct hit (***opposite***) and four people were trapped in the rubble. The Westminster Bank adjoining was also badly damaged and windows (including no doubt Lord Bristol's) shattered over a wide area. The Caledonian Club, on the south side of Charles II St, had to evacuate after further damage a few weeks later, and went to lodge at the East India across the Square, though that too had lost windows.[12]

The great raids of May 1941 brought more destruction, but the most potentially devastating attack occurred as late as February 1944, when a stick of bombs fell on a diagonal line from near Christie's in King St to Mason's Yard, doing sad damage to the rear parts of the historic houses on the West side of the Square. The London Library suffered worst of all and Mr Lees-Milne remembered forming part of a human chain of salvagers – 'stood on a girder projecting from a wall and threw books from the theological department to a neighbour'.[13] A staff member, Miss Joan Bailey, recalls coming in the next morning and finding the then librarian, Mr C. J. Purnell, and his wife (almost full-time fire-watchers), standing forlorn amidst a wilderness of rubble, splintered woodwork and savaged books. Had the track of these bombs been 50 yards further to the east, the losses to the Square would have been incalculable.

Harking back to that 1941 AGM, Lord Strafford (sole Trustee present in this and two subsequent years), also considered a 'renewed' request by the Ministry of Supply for the removal of the Square railings as scrap. The railings went – 18 tons, 3 cwt of them – and a singularly mild compensation claim of £22 13*s* 9*d* was lodged.

From then onwards, the story is one of utilitarian pressure on the garden, its

57. Second World War – direct hit on No. 2 (14 October 1940).

visual charm forgotten for the 'duration'. King William's statue had already disappeared, having been spirited away by the Ministry of Works on February 14 1941 for safekeeping at Berkhamsted Castle.[14] That this was a wise precaution is shown by the fact that one bomb (which fortunately failed to explode) fell only a few yards south of the empty plinth.

'Digging for victory' became inevitable and seems to have had a particular attraction for Court jewellers. At any rate, during 1942 'allotments' were let to Messrs Asprey, of New Bond St, and Messrs Garrard, of Grafton St, at nominal rentals of 1*s* per annum; this was in addition to the large area occupied by the Auxiliary Fire Service. Judging by subsequent War Damage claims, both the War Office (which offered a modest £425 in compensation) and the RAF made use of part of the garden, and in fact there are references to a 'road' constructed by the latter, though it is far from clear what they were doing there.

Traces of another aspect of the 'war effort' are still perceptible in St James's Square today. This was the extreme demand for office accommodation by military and civilian Government Departments. At the outbreak of war, there was no such 'presence' in the Square; by the end of it, Nos. 4, 5, 6, 7, 8, 12, 13, 19, 31 (Norfolk House) and 32/33 were all under requisition. The North side indeed (5–8, 12, 13) was almost monopolized by the Ministry of Labour and National Service, thanks to the expansionist leadership of Ernest Bevin; it also patched up the old Caledonian Club premises at Nos. 32 and 33. Nos. 4 and 31 were put to

58. The 6th Earl of Strafford and Countess. A 'conversation piece' by Sir William Nicholson.

more glamorous use, the Astors' mansion being taken over by the Free French in 1943, while Norfolk House won fame as General Eisenhower's London headquarters before the invasions of North Africa and Europe – mention has already been made of the plaque which records the fact.

One of the few houses which fulfilled a wartime function while remaining in private hands was No. 11. Having been a centre of work for prisoners of war in 1914–18, it now sheltered the Committee for War Refugees, with Lady Iveagh again the driving force. Refugees arrived in great numbers and since many of them brought nothing but a small suitcase, they had to be clothed as well as fed and housed. Inevitably, they were a mixed bunch from a variety of Continental countries, and at one time No. 11 was positively infested with military and civil police expecting to sniff out Fifth Columnists.

* * *

VE Day came at last, but the return to something like normality was slow in St James's Square. A landmark was the reinstatement of King William's statue on April 15 1946. In the same month the Trustees (with Lord Strafford still in the chair) invited Mr R. F. G. Saunders, of the East India Club, and Mr Ivison Macadam, of the Royal Institute of International Affairs, to join them, and immediately deputed the latter to consult the Ministry of Works about a suitable firm to rehabilitate the garden. At an extra meeting in July it was decided to give the job to Messrs Landscape Ltd. Their original estimate had been about £4000, but 'after considering the matter with Lord Strafford', they slimmed this down to £2116, of which it was thought £145 could be charged to Westminster City Council in respect of the shelters (in the end the Council paid £262 10*s*).

The temporary palings were replaced by Messrs Boulton & Paul with a somewhat less unsightly chain link fence (costing £291 17*s* 8*d*), the gate then existing at the south-west corner being omitted. So far so good, but the problem of a more permanent restoration of the perimeter of the garden was merely being shelved and would have contentious consequences, as we shall see.

De-requisitioning was a costive process and did not gather any pace until the 1950s, when Nos. 31 (Norfolk House), 32 and the upper part of 33 were relinquished,[15] as well as Nos. 5 and 6 on the North side. The Ministry of Employment, however, retained a tenacious hold on Nos. 7 and 8 (where the Minister had his office), thus causing the Square to be the focus of press activity – and occasional 'demos' – during recurrent crises of industrial unrest. Nos. 12 and 13 had been linked by the same Ministry, but in 1952 the National Bank of India (predecessors to the present Grindlays) moved into No. 13. No. 12 was afterwards joined to No. 11 instead, and drew further public attention as the headquarters of the Advisory Conciliation and Arbitration Service (ACAS) for many years to come.

XV
A Last Look Round

In spite of the ravages of war, which we have noted, and of redevelopment, to which we shall revert, St James's Square emerged into the 1950s with a respectable amount of its architectural heritage intact, and remains so today. This is shown by the fact that no fewer than seventeen of the twenty-five houses on the West, North and East sides are 'listed' under the Town and Country Planning Act (1971) as retaining features – outside or in – of special importance. They are graded as follows:

Nos.	Grade	Nos.	Grade
4	Grade II*	15	Grade I
5	Grade II	16	Grade II
7	Grade II	18	Grade II
9	Grade II*	20	Grade I
10	Grade I	21	Grade II*
11	Grade II*	31a	Grade II
12	Grade II*	32	Grade II*
13	Grade II*	33	Grade II*
14	Grade II		

*Grade II buildings of particular value.

In addition, King William's statue is classified under Grade I and the Summer House Grade II.

Of the buildings failing to qualify for the above list, we have already noted the fate of old Norfolk House (No. 31), demolished and rebuilt in the late 1930s.[1] Nos. 1 and 2 fell victims to bombing (the latter being completely destroyed) and were subsequently replaced after a somewhat anonymous fashion (*'retardaire'* – Pevsner) by Messrs Mewès & Davis. The National Westminster Bank resumed its long occupation of the lower part of No. 1 and eventually the advertising firm of D'Arcy MacManus Masius[1] took over No. 2 and also spread over the Bank.

No. 3 had been one of the first targets for redevelopment, being pulled down as long ago as 1930. Because it faced an 'open space', the architects for its replacement, Messrs Ospalek, were unfortunately allowed to ignore the height limitation to 80 ft, first mentioned in connection with Norfolk House (p. 64). So the new No. 3 rose to over 100 ft, and though it was given a would-be Georgian dress, its sixth-floor arcade and the attic storey on top of that provide perhaps the Square's worst 'sore thumb', particularly in relation to its low-built neighbours, Nos. 4 and 5. This is only partially redeemed by Mr Newbury Trent's pleasant carvings of 'London Street Cries' just above street level.

No. 6 was rebuilt by the respected architectural partnership of Fitzroy Robinson, as the outcome of a redevelopment wrangle of quite remarkable complexity. This followed the ending of the historic Hervey occupation in 1955, and it would not be profitable to pursue it through all its ramifications. Briefly, however, by 1957 the 6th Earl of Strafford's daughter, Lady Elizabeth Byng, was in possession of No. 6 as well as the old Byng mansion and applied for planning permission to demolish both. This was granted for No. 6, but a Preservation Order was placed on the two lower floors of No. 5. A scheme was put forward for the rest of the two houses to be rebuilt as offices, with a way through from No. 6 to No. 5's 'state' rooms. The development was to be carried out by Messrs F. Minter, but in the event the freehold of No. 6 was sold to Sir Charles Clore; after further permutations the house was pulled down and the Fitzroy Robinson office block replaced it. Consolidated Zinc Corporation took a lease and in 1975 its successor, Rio Tinto Zinc ('RTZ') became freeholders. Members of the Byng family retained their interest in No. 5 for a while longer, but eventually that ancient freehold passed to a property company and thence to the Libyan Government, with the traumatic results which will be the subject of our epilogue.

Moving on to No. 8, redevelopment followed immediately upon the amalgamation of the Sports Club with the East India in 1938 and the migration of its members to the West side of the Square. Here again *height* became an issue, but in this instance the applicants, Messrs Robert Angell & Curtis, were forbidden to exceed the 80 ft limit. So in the course of 1939 the present office building went up; it was almost immediately taken over by the Ministry of Labour which, as we have seen, remained in possession until the 1960s.

One demolition plan which fortunately came to nought related to Nos. 9 and 10, forming the other St James's Square/Duke of York St corner. For the origins of this proposal we have to go back as far as May 1919, when the late Lionel

59. No. 3, detail of the frieze 'Street Cries of London'. Newbury Trent.

Curtis suggested to a meeting of British and American delegations to the Paris Peace Conference that a new permanent body was needed for the study of international relations. This led to the inauguration a year later of what was then called the British Institute of International Affairs. It occupied various temporary roosts, but in 1923 had the chance to buy No. 10, following the death of Lord Kinnaird. A Canadian supporter, Col. R. W. Leonard, operating behind the scenes, advanced £42,000 for the purchase of the freehold and another £8000 for conversion. The opening took place on November 9 1923, with Lord Grey of Falloden in the chair and in the presence of the Prince of Wales and an imposing array of Commonwealth statesmen. By now the organization had been rechristened the Royal Institute for the Study of International and Commonwealth Affairs, but soon became better known as Chatham House, in honour of the first of No. 10's three Prime Ministers.

Curiously enough, World War II gave a big boost to international studies and No. 10 became overcrowded with courses for members of the fighting services and others. Lord Astor, as Chairman, enlisted the powerful help of the Foreign Secretary, Anthony Eden, as the result of which negotiations with the Portland Club for the purchase of No. 9 next door were completed in 1943 at a cost of £50,000.

Forward now to 1959. Nos. 9 and 10 were a pair of fine old mansions, but in spite of alterations and additions never proved ideal for the Institute's purposes. So came about the proposal to demolish and rebuild them, while possibly retaining some internal features. In the event, Preservation Orders were placed on both.

This completes our tale of visible reconstruction on the East and North sides of the Square. On the West, we have already noted the masterly duplication by Messrs Mewès & Davis of the Adam façade of No. 20, when the Distillers' Company took over the site of No. 21. Very different was the fate of the curious late Victorian structure substituted for old Cleveland House (No. 19) on the southern corner of King St. It was in its turn demolished in and replaced in 1966 by what is so far the Square's main specimen of 'modern' architectural idiom (Chapman Taylor & Partners). Opinions about it may differ, but it somehow seems no more unneighbourly than neo-Georgianism on the East side.

Thus the present somewhat uneasy equilibrium between past and present was reached in St James's Square, and with the current emphasis on 'conservation', it is hard to imagine further drastic changes in the near future. But though it has been Government policy for over a quarter of a century to discourage any intensification of office development in the area, this has not prevented some grandiose schemes being mooted. Representative of these was a 1961 proposal covering nearly an acre on the West side. While retaining the 'listed' façades and some rooms behind them, two parallel eight-storey buildings were to be erected on parts of the sites of Nos. 14 (London Library), 15 (Clerical, Medical), 16/17 (East India Club) and 18 (Hawker Siddeley House), together with various rear premises in Duke St. A lot of hard work was done on this (see *Foursome in St James's*, op. cit., pp. 148–50), but, not surprisingly, the official reply was No.

* * *

Meanwhile, in the centre, the perimeter of the garden retained something of its shabby 'bomb site' look. It was not until their January 1963 meeting that the Trustees decided to sound the Ministry of Labour (presumably because the then Minister, John Hare, had already shown an interest in the garden) on the prospects of achieving a 'more elegant enclosure'. Meanwhile it was agreed that, for reasons of cost, it would not be feasible to replace the old wrought-iron railings unless a benefactor could be found. None came forward, however, and in May 1967 the same phrase, 'a more elegant enclosure', surfaced once more, this time with a faint suggestion of support from the Civic Trust. Two years later it was at least decided not to replace the old chain-link fence with a plastic-covered one, but to try to build up funds for something more dignified.

Eventually (July 21 1972), came the first momentous hint of a possible handover of the garden to Westminster City Council. The Chairman of the Trustees by then was Mr J. B. H. Pegler (Clerical, Medical), and papers which he now circulated showed that he and Mr S. G. Gillam (London Library) had been talking to the Deputy City Solicitor about the legal and financial implications. By way of background, the City Engineer had provided an estimate of just over £15,000 for a complete replacement of the perimeter wall and fence, to be reduced to only £4000 if plastic-covered chain-link were to be substituted for new wrought-iron railings and brick piers 'to the City Council's pattern for the London Squares'.

From that moment onwards a sharp and at times almost acrimonious division of opinion emerged. It hinged in part on the ever-interesting question of who actually owned (and owns) the soil of the garden. This had been more or less dormant since the early nineteenth century, when the Trustees made determined efforts to settle it in their own favour. At their January 29 1819 meeting, for example, the Clerk reported on a conference with the Earl of Hardwicke, who had referred to the 'mistaken' opinion that the soil was vested in the surviving Trustee of the Earl of St Albans, and it was agreed to apply to the Crown for a formal grant. The Crown Commissioners, however, took the view that only Parliament could act, and thereafter the story for several years was of successive attempts to smuggle the Trustees' 'rights' into some appropriate Act. These seem to have collapsed in about 1822, when it was reported that having missed the bus with the Crown Revenue Bill, Mr George Byng, MP, promised to 'talk to Mr Huskisson about the next Bill relevant to the Land Revenues of the Crown'.

The Royal Commission of 1924 certainly assumed that the Trustees were the freeholders, but among Mr Pegler's July 1972 dossier was a learned contribution by his colleague, Mr H. N. Beetlestone, which threw doubt on their very existence as a legal entity, in the light of what the Act of 1824 laid down about their qualifications and powers. His own final and 'startling' conclusion was that the garden was probably common land as defined by Section 2(i) of the Commons Registration Act 1965 and should have been registered as such before March 1 1970. The only solution might be to declare that as the Square could no longer be maintained by a rate within the limits of the 1726 Act, the latter was now a spent force. If so, this would let in the Town Gardens Protection Act of 1863 and Westminster City Council could be required to take action.

Nobody liked the 'common' idea much, and henceforward both the City Council and the majority of the Trustees seem to have made up their minds that the soil of the garden was in fact Crown property, though this came to be challenged later. More immediately, at their meeting on November 6 1972, the Trustees agreed to be represented by Mr Pegler and Mr K. Smith (Dept of Employment) at any future negotiations with the Council. From this, only Mr J. Gledhill (East India Club), making his last appearance as a Trustee, dissented. The torch, however, was taken up by his successor, Mr 'Pat' Wallace, who for some time acted as a sort of one-man rebel group, both challenging the assumption by the Crown and the City Council that the former owned the freehold, and opposing the repeal of the 1726 Act. Gradually, support grew up[3] for the idea that the future of the garden would be better safeguarded by the

Trustees themselves than if it were 'municipalized', even with the best intentions. Memoranda flew to and fro, special meetings were convened and finally on March 19 1974 a resolution that the Trustees should 'continue management of the garden' was carried by 8 votes to 7. The Chairman resigned and was succeeded, inevitably, by the chief dissident, Mr Wallace.

Money of course was now the problem. However, the new Chairman was soon able to announce that no less than £15,800 had been donated or promised to help in the reinstatement of the wall and railings, and that a new voluntary rate would ensure an income of £4500 for three years. The Trustees were not totally out of the wood – there is in front of us a 29-item schedule of letters and meetings during the twelve months ending January 31 1976, concerned with (a) Planning permission for the project,(b) The possibilities of grant aid from the Department of the Environment, the Greater London and Westminster City Councils, *et alia*. Out of all this emerged the offer of a GLC grant of £750 – a meagre enough return for the Trustees' successive modifications of their plans to suit what they no doubt regarded as bureaucratic fads and fancies.

By 1974 the present handsome gates and railings had been installed, but there was no intention that they should exclude the general public from reasonable enjoyment of the garden. It had in fact been open in the lunch hour since the early 1950s and now a much wider access was conceded, as the current notice shows:

> These PRIVATE GARDENS,[4] which are open to the public Monday to Friday 10 a.m. to 4.30 p.m., are administered by the St James's Square Trustees, who are solely responsible for their maintenance. The co-operation of all users in keeping them tidy will be greatly appreciated.

In addition to dealing with the perimeter, the new Chairman and his colleagues devoted much time and all the money they could spare to improving the garden itself, with delightful results. It is fortunate that physical alterations to its layout and contents have always been conservative. One recalls that what the Trustees regarded as unsuitable offers of a birdbath from Mr Wakefield MP and of a 'statue' from the East India Club[5] were tactfully fended off in the 1950s, and the four stone obelisks (p. 148) which since 1985 have grouped themselves round King William's statue, actually hark back to the eight which framed the original enclosure. In themselves, they are part of a scheme, including a circle of rose beds, planned by Mr John Brookes, to give the statue an even worthier setting. It was during excavations for the erection of the obelisks that the solid flint bottom of the former basin 4 ft down was revealed (p. 35).

As enjoyed by the walker or lounger of today, the garden represents an almost perfect balance of nature and artifice – 'space, light, grateful shadow, gentle grandeur', as that *Times* writer described it, sixty-six years ago. Dominant, of course, are the great London Planes, more than a dozen of them, though of varying ages: the largest, it is thought, could well date from that moment in June 1873 when Lords Bristol and Derby 'marked out sites' for additional plantings.

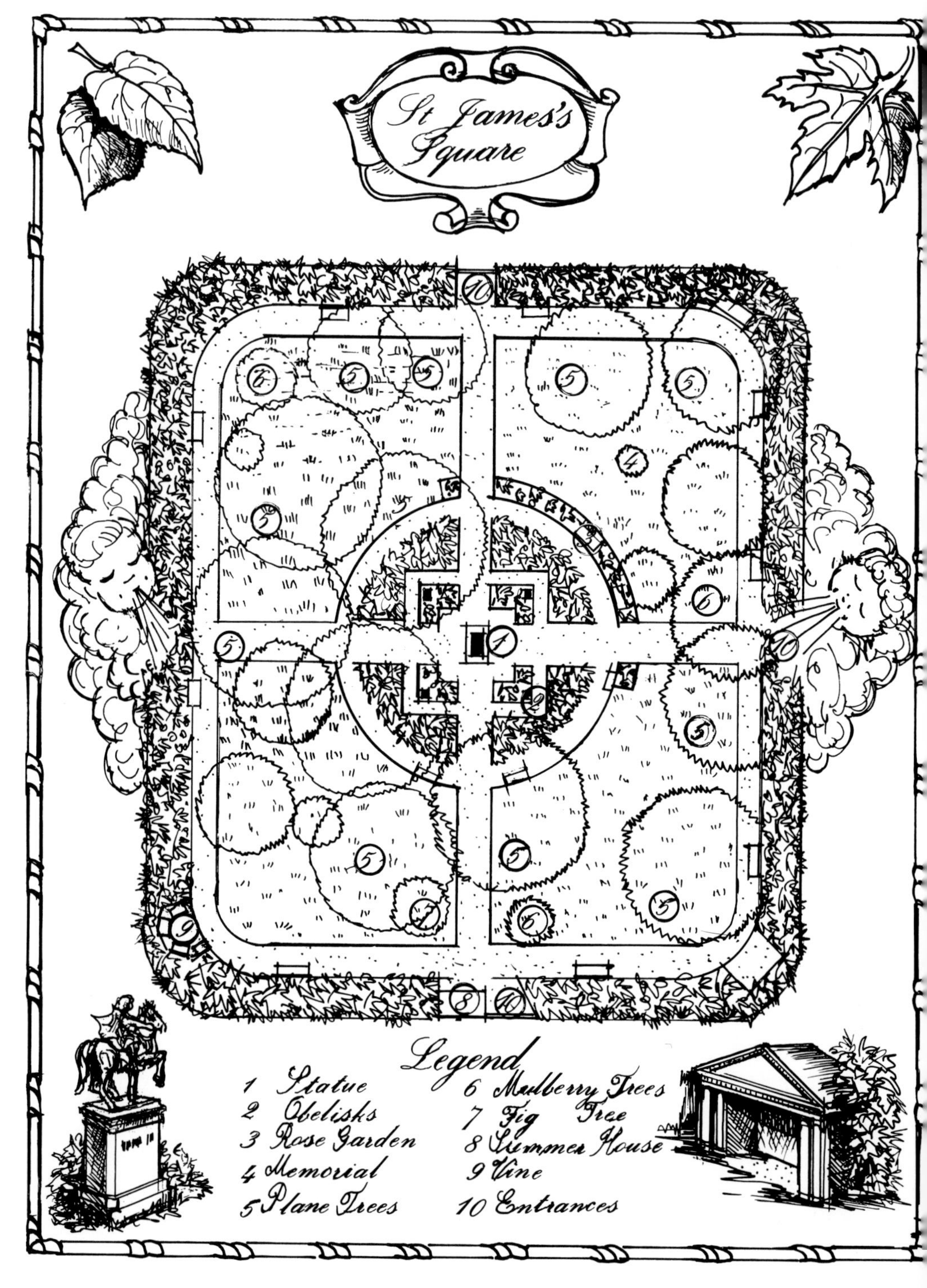

60. The garden, 1986.

Up to twenty other species lend support, notable among them Hawthorn, Lime, Catalpa, Tree of Heaven, Mulberry and Fig. The two Mulberries one would like to salute as descendants of those which the Stuart Kings nurtured so lovingly in St James's; at the moment, one is erect, the other prostrate, yet it is the latter that (as the present writer can gratefully testify) continues from time to time to furnish the raw material for delicious mulberry tart. The solitary Fig, on the other hand, for all its Medusa-like writhings, finds it difficult to bring its fruit to maturity.

Shrubs have recently begun to make a fine showing, no longer 'shabby' or 'grimy' as of old. They cover over 100 varieties, of which the following deserve to be noted:

Amelanchier canadensis	(Snowy Mespilis)
Arundinaria nitida	(Bamboo)
Aucuba japonica variegata	(Spotted Laurel)
Buddleia davidii	(Butterfly Bush)
Ceanothus impressus	
Cornus alba Elegantissima	(Variegated Dogwood)
Corylus maxima menma Purpurea	(Purple Leaf Filbert)
Fatsia japonica	(Japanese Aralia)
Garrya elliptica	(Silk Tassel)
Ilex altaclarensis Golden King	(Variegated Holly)
Magnolia stellata	(Star Magnolia)
Mahonia bealei	
Philadelphus microphyllus	(Mock Orange)
Phormium tenax	(New Zealand Flax)
Rhododendron luteum	
Viburnum opulus	(Guelder Rose)

Finally, at ground level we are offered some twenty different roses, herbaceous and climbing plants in variety and, as spring breaks through, a heart-warming display of daffodils and other bulbs.

So much leafage brings its problems, of course. Ever since the garden was created, the 'smoke nuisance' from autumnal leaf-burning has been a cause of contention, and despite the periodic attempts of Chairmen to evade it by artfully shifting the bonfires from one quarter of the garden to another, complaints – and even the intervention of Environmental Health – continue to this day. Much of the leaf-fall, of course, goes onto the compost heap, but for this too there is only limited space.

In past times, full-time gardeners were in charge. Then came contractors of varying efficiency, but since 1976 there has been a gardener once more (John Callan), with a professional landscapist (Roger Storr) to advise on planting, pruning, lopping and so on.

Lopping, indeed (as carried out with some necessary severity early in 1986) tends to provoke the cry so familiar to those in charge of public or semi-public open spaces – 'What about the birds?' It is time that these particular denizens of the garden had their niche in our chronicle, and we are not just talking about sparrows, starlings, pigeons, as the casual observer might suppose. Letter received by the Trustees in March 1986:

> Can I firstly say thank you for providing a beautiful Square to have my lunch or just walk through for some fresh air.
>
> In my lunchtimes I have become aware of the abundant bird life living in the Square – a family of wrens (they had 6 young ones last year), a robin, blackbirds, thrushes, dunnock, blue tits, great tits, finches. I have attempted during this winter to feed them when I could and I am sure many other people do likewise.

The writer goes on to plead for more cover both in winter and for spring nest-building, and perhaps some water also, to improve the birds' environment, and she ends as she began – 'Again I thank you – it is a lovely Square'.[6]

It is at dusk, perhaps, that the magic of St James's Square and its garden is at its most compelling, above all if one pauses outside the railings to the west and gazes past the leaf-embowered statue and down the long vista to the pillared portico of Nash's Haymarket Theatre. Magic of a different sort, too, on those festive evenings when the foliage is illuminated by the gas flambeaux along the front of the East India Club; they date from the 1860s and have been justly described as 'perhaps the earliest and certainly the most poetic form of flood-lighting ever invented'.

Naturally, the garden itself remains a popular setting for the receptions, and even the occasional open-air play, put on by the neighbours. There have been suggestions, especially when the Arts Council was still at No. 4, that it would be an ideal arena for sculpture exhibitions. One particularly glittering prospect was held out in 1975 – a display of works by the late Henry Moore OM. On the precedent of the great exhibition in Florence not long before, it was thought that at least 175,000 people might attend, and that after the cost of rehabilitating the garden after such an invasion, a substantial sum might be raised for charity. However, the plan foundered on the objections of Mr Moore himself; after a walk round he seems to have decided that the trees were too competitive – 'Sculptures in themselves'!

An ambitious scheme which did come off was the extravaganza by the Jermyn Street Association in conjunction with the Junior Variety Club of Great Britain on the evening of September 12 1985. Over £50,000 was raised for the club's charity. But because it went on into the early hours, it also raised some hackles among adjacent club dwellers – a caution for the future. No such complaints about the band concert (the first ever held in the Square) which a few days earlier celebrated the 400th anniversary of the City of Westminster.

The question of rehabilitation is always very much in the Trustees' minds when agreeing terms for 'happenings' in the garden. Just one example of how maintenance costs can multiply. In the year 1871 Bishop Wilberforce and Mr Tollemache were given the grave responsibility of choosing between tenders of £27 10*s* and £30 for painting the railings. By the 1930s the cost had approximately doubled; the latest tender is £6500. It is fortunate that the number as well as the commitment of the Trustees has increased since the decision to maintain the Square's independence. While the Statutory Rate has remained anchored at its immemorial 10*s* (or 50p) per foot of frontage, yielding a derisory £608 per annum, in 1985 the Voluntary Rate which the owners or tenants are prepared to levy on themselves reached a total of £12,825. This was modestly supplemented by £150 from 'key-holders' (mainly occupants of flats in the old Junior Carlton building).

* * *

All this owes much to the two most recent Chairmen – Mr Wallace, whose leadership in the events of 1973–74 we have already noted, and Mr Dennis Hill, Managing Director of Winchester House Property Co.,[7] who took over in 1982. It was in Mr Wallace's time, incidentally, that a change was made in the Clerkship to the Trustees, an office held since as long ago as 1822 by the firm of Dixey & Co. and ultimately by its successors, Messrs Dearden, Lord, Annan, Morrish. From 1974 onwards the work has been done by the Chairman's staff, the current Clerk being Mr Brian Russell.

The support given to the Voluntary Rate (as well as to such projects as the present volume) reflects in part the final evolution of the whole St James's district from a residential to a business quarter of London. In spite of the many losses we have recorded, what is left of old St James's Square is being well looked after by its inheritors. The current method of trying to make the original buildings viable is to restore and maintain any surviving 'state' apartments, while providing additional office space above and/or behind. This is just what we saw the Iveagh Trust doing at No. 11 (p. 51); the most recent example is No. 33,[8] where the property firm of Hammersons took a long lease in 1983 and proceeded to erect a more or less invisible seven-storey office block to the east. The fine Adam and Soane rooms facing the Square and Charles II St were brought back to their pristine condition and then the whole thing was taken over by Messrs Consolidated Gold Fields.

Clubs and 'institutions' now occupy no more than half a dozen houses, though an interesting recent arrival is the Royal Fine Arts Commission. It has been 'decanted' into No. 7 to facilitate other departmental moves elsewhere, but is likely to find its permanent home there. Indeed, what better use could be made of Sir Edwin Lutyens' legacy to St James's Square?

In painful contrast has been the fate of that historic mansion, No. 4. Once it had come into the possession of the Astor family (p. 132), they used it non-stop for entertaining guests who ranged from T. E. Lawrence and Sean O'Casey to Gandhi, Neville Chamberlain and Ribbentrop, while the neighbours became accustomed to the vision of the redoubtable Nancy Astor doing her exercises or rehearsing her speeches on the back balcony. Following the Free French occupancy during World War II, there were one or two other official tenants, and then in 1948 Lord Astor sold the house to HM Government at what was

61. No. 20, the Ante-room by Robert Adam; later Lady Elizabeth Bowes-Lyon's schoolroom.

described as an 'advantageous' price, so that it could be restored as a West End showcase for the Arts Council.

Many will have memories of passing up the noble staircase to enjoy a rich succession of exhibitions in the first-floor rooms. However, No. 4 did not work nearly so well as an administrative headquarters; in 1968 the Council moved out and, amid sharp controversy in which the Chairman of the Trustees, Lieut-Colonel Geoffrey Kup, became involved,[9] the beautiful old house was converted into a Crown Court. This was presented as merely a temporary measure, but there was no great improvement from a public access point of view when, after a few years, the Court was succeeded by the present Employment Appeals Tribunal. The main features of the interior are preserved, albeit behind partitions in some cases, but the tale is a cautionary one which needs to be put on record.

* * *

The impulse is strong, in a book like this, to keep harking back to the past, and as we come towards a close there is every temptation to do so just once more in the company of someone to whom St James's Square still represents youth and happiness three-quarters of a century ago.

We have already quoted some of the memories which visits to No. 20 have revived for Her Majesty Queen Elizabeth the Queen Mother. Still others surfaced when on December 12 1985 she returned to meet members of the Royal Warrant Holders' Association. This time she recalled in particular the epoch when she graduated from the second-floor nurseries to the school-room below – none other in fact than the small but beautifully decorated apartment (opposite) which Robert Adam designed as the prologue to his two great 'withdrawing-rooms'. Here the young Lady Elizabeth did her lessons and began to entertain her friends; from her point of view the only slight disadvantage of the room was that it had a canopied balcony (since removed) over the front-door, where she was persuaded to have breakfast rather publicly 'for her health's sake'. It may well have been from this balcony that she heard strains of 'jazz music' drifting across from the garden during World War I – the source, no doubt, Washington Inn (p. 134).

Apart from the mild embarrassment of breakfasting *coram populo*, No. 20 St James's Square seems to have been a secure and charming place in which to grow up – even the ghost whom Lady Elizabeth's sister once encountered in the corridor near the school-room took the benignant form of a handsome young man in eighteenth-century costume!

One could wish to end on this note of happy reminiscence. Unfortunately there is still one more episode to be chronicled, which brought the Square into hideous confrontation with the realities of life in the 1980s.

Epilogue

One April Day . . .

The return of the *corps diplomatique* – absent from St James's Square for over 200 years – became progressively less likely as our century advanced, and when it did occur it was not in a particularly welcome form. The 'Libyan People's Bureau', which took over No. 5 in 1975, may have had diplomatic status, but its very title seemed to compromise this, while the massive steel grilles which immediately appeared over every window were also a sinister portent. And indeed there followed rumours of an internal 'coup' whereby an extreme group was supposed to have usurped power from the more orthodox representatives originally posted to London by Colonel Gaddafi.

Periodical 'demos' seemed inevitable, and local office staffs were only mildly interested when on the morning of April 17 1984 some seventy people gathered in the north-east corner of the Square. Many of them wore masks and carried banners inscribed 'Gaddafi Hangs Students!', and slogans were shouted to the same effect. The police (present in some force) carefully shepherded them towards the central footway, while confining a small group of pro-Gaddafi demonstrators to an area outside Nos. 2 and 3. Everything in fact seemed under control, but suddenly everything changed. There was a burst of gunfire lasting about ten seconds, a young policewoman called Yvonne Fletcher was seen to fall and her blood poured from a stomach wound onto the roadway. Colleagues, including her fiancé PC Michael Liddle, gathered round her and she was rushed to Westminster Hospital where, in spite of frantic work by the surgeons, she died within an hour. Several of the demonstrators were also wounded.

Eye-witnesses soon established that the source of the shots was the Libyan People's Bureau and that they were almost certainly fired from a second-floor window. The Square was quickly cleared, and soon all that there was to be seen was WPC Fletcher's hat lying pathetically in the road along with the helmets of several of her comrades.

And now ensued what all the world soon heard of as 'the siege of St James's Square'. Nobody knew just how many people had been involved in the outrage, or whether a break-out from the Embassy (as we may for convenience call No. 5) would be attempted. In any case, all the approaches to the Square were sealed off, an operations room was set up in No. 2 and marksmen were posted on roof tops and (incongruously enough) among the daffodils of the Square garden. It gradually emerged, however, that for reasons which the public hardly appreciated, there was to be no attempt to storm the building or to arrest the murderers. And so at last on April 28, thirty men emerged from the front door with their hands above their heads and were whisked off to an interrogation centre and thence to Heathrow and a waiting Libyan plane.

It must be admitted that, once the initial feeling of horror had worn off, the 'siege' did provide an interlude of adventure for people still authorized to work in the Square. With the roads and footpaths blocked, unorthodox approaches had to be worked out, often reversing an original evacuation route such as (in one typical case) 'through the roof door, over the roofs, along the catwalks, down about 25 ft of extension ladders, across the next roof and eventually down eight flights of stairs'. And this being England, there was the inevitable story of the recce party, gaining admission to their building after several days, being urgently briefed – 'for God's sake feed the goldfish'.

The emergency passed, but Yvonne Fletcher was not forgotten. People's hearts had been touched by the tiny figure of this young girl – she was only 5 ft 2½ ins. tall, but the height regulations had been waived in view of her determination since childhood to join the Force. The Trustees of St James's Square felt that the best possible memorial would be a flowering tree, planted in the garden near the scene of the outrage, and in this they had the support of the Fletcher family and of Yvonne's colleagues at Vine St and Bow St.

However, at that point a divergence occurred. Mr Michael Winner, a film producer, had been putting a great deal of energy into an organization called the Police Memorial Trust, and not long after the Square Trustees' decision about the tree, he came forward with the idea of a second memorial, carved in stone. This was to be mounted on the retaining wall of the garden opposite No. 5, a part of the railings being cut away for the purpose. The Square Trustees had reservations about this, the matter got into the Press and accusations of hard-heartedness were flung about. Eventually the controversy simmered down, but one could heartily wish it had never occurred.

On Wednesday November 21 the tree, a pink cherry (*Prunus shirofugen*), was duly planted at a quiet ceremony in the presence of Yvonne Fletcher's parents

62. Tree planting ceremony in memory of WPC Yvonne Fletcher, 21 November 1984.

and many of the local police, headed by Chief-Superintendent Kendrick, and was blessed by the Rector of St James's, Piccadilly, the Rev. Donald Reeve. 'A lovely way to remember her,' said Mrs Fletcher.

Then on February 1 1985 came a grander public commemoration when the Prime Minister, supported by the leaders of all the political parties and many other dignitaries, unveiled the Police Memorial Trust's stone, which had eventually been sited at pavement level.

And ever since then offerings of flowers have continued to recall the April day when St James's Square – never, in all its long history, totally immune from violence – became fully caught up in the horrors of our time.

Postscript 2001

Fourteen years have elapsed since the first edition of the St James's Square book was published. The Trustees have decided to produce a second edition, and this postscript attempts to bring our readers up to date with happenings in the Gardens and surrounding area.

Sadly, the author, Denys Forrest, died five years ago. The Trustees are indebted to him for the excellent volume that he produced which took him some eighteen months of extensive research, and they are justifiably proud of the finished result.

The Gardens continue to be run in the format as described in Chapter 15.

National Westminster bank who occupied Nos. 1 and 2, St James's Square, made the momentous decision to leave the square after a bank presence on that site for 140 years. An application was made by them for the construction of a new building on the site and after extended negotiation with Westminster City Council approval was granted. Approval was conditional on the National Westminster bank contributing £100,000 towards the local environment (The Gardens).

This prompted the Trustees to appoint a landscape architect in the form of the Colson Stone Partnership to produce a paper on how best to spend the money.

Colson Stone submitted a full report tracing the history of the landscaping of the Gardens together with recommendations on improvements that should be undertaken within the budget set. Their conclusion was to bring the Gardens back to an eighteenth-century design, by stripping out all central planting, obelisks and paths and creating lawns surrounding the statue of William III, thus bringing the Monarch back to the focal point of the garden. In addition, the Nash Grade II listed summerhouse would be surrounded by the gardens by repositioning the south access gate to the East. All the perimeter planting would be increased to achieve a natural barrier between the garden and surrounding roadway.

After numerous delays in planning, approval for this scheme was eventually granted in the middle of 1999. Tenders were sought and a contract was granted to LDC Ltd of Woking, Surrey in October 1999. Work commenced in January 2000 and was completed in May 2000.

It will take some time for the perimeter planting to establish itself, but already the effect is evident, an eighteenth-century garden, dominated, as it was intended, by the magnificent statue of William III.

City & West End property company have kindly donated a full-size bronze statue of a stag to the Trustees. This has been created by the sculptor Marcus Cornish and will be positioned in the south-west corner of the gardens early in 2001.

At the Annual General Meeting in May 2000, Dennis Hill, who had been a Trustee since 1968, and Chairman for over thirteen years in two separate terms, retired, John Stevens of the Naval & Military Club (now situated at No. 4 St James's Square) was appointed Chairman. At the same time Dennis Hill was appointed honorary President of the Trust and Penny Kennedy Scott is now Clerk of the Trust.

John Callan, the gardener, has now been joined by his brother, Brian and they jointly keep the garden in good order, assisted by George Boon. LDC Ltd of Woking now handle the specialised garden work on a regular basis.

A list of the names of the current Trustees appears under Appendix 1a.

Many changes have occurred in the occupancy and ownership of the buildings around the Square. Under Appendix II in the original edition, a detailed description of each building appeared. Appendix IIa shows the up-to-date occupancy of each building and, where applicable, details of new buildings which have been constructed since the 1986 edition (Nos. 1 & 2, No. 18, No. 19 and Nos. 20 & 21).

The Trustees hope that everyone visiting the Gardens enjoy their beauty and appreciate the new layout.

Notes

Chapter I The Bailiwick of St James

(1) *Henrietta Maria* (London, Hodder & Stoughton, 1936), p. 170. Jermyn was then, according to Miss Oman, 'a large, heavy, fair young man with a sleepy eye, the shoulders of a drayman, not many brains and a mordant sense of humour'.
(2) This particular phrase derives from Pepys (Diary, December 31 1662), but the evidence for a child, and even for a marriage, is scanty and unreliable. Gossip a-plenty – no hard facts. See also Sir John Reresby, *Memoirs*, ed. A. Browning (Glasgow, Jackson, 1931), p. 29.
(3) For a discussion of the game of *paille-maille* (a sort of air-borne croquet) and the alleys devoted to it, see *Survey of London* (Athlone Press for the London County Council, 1960), vol. XXIX, p. 115. Henceforward quoted as *Survey*.
(4) For some of the issues involved, see D. M. Forrest, *The Oriental* (London, Batsford, rev. ed., 1979), p. 154 *et seq*.
(5) Christopher Simon Sykes, *Private Palaces* (London, Chatto & Windus, 1985).
(6) The surname and title of King Charles's Secretary of State are nowadays commemorated to the west of St James's St.
(7) No. 17 now absorbed, with 16, into the East India Club (p. 108).
(8) Denounced as a Jacobite after the death of Queen Anne, he fled abroad in 1715 and never returned. For its last years before the 1719 sale, Ormonde House remained in the hands of the exiled Duke's brother, the unassuming old Earl of Arran.
(9) *Diary*, July 13 1663.
(10) 'Squinting but rich', she was at one time thought of as a suitable bride for John Churchill.
(11) For the later vicissitudes of No. 21, see Chapter VI.

Chapter II The Last of the Jermyns

(1) Quoted by the *Survey of London* from Robert Seymour, *A Survey of the Cities of London and Westminster* (1735), vol. II, p. 663.
(2) Narcissus Luttrell, *Brief Historical Relation of State Affairs* (reprinted Oxford, 1857), vol. 2, pp. 250–51.
(3) Horace Walpole told Horace Mann (letter of December 6 1783) that 'our mitred Proteus' had the previous year let his house 'at a usurious £700 a year' without telling his wife.
(4) *Survey of London* (op. cit. above).
(5) For a fuller account, see D. M. Forrest, *Foursome in St James's* (East India, Devonshire, Sports and Public Schools' Club, 1982), pp. 49–50.

Chapter III 'The Great Square Place'

(1) Printed in Dasent (Appendix B).
(2) She had been married under duress, being already in love with Prince Charles of Lorrain. On the second night of her marriage to Cosmo she tried 'by endearments and threats' to get her hands on the Medici crown jewels, then the richest in the world. She soon showed undisguised aversion to her husband and there were allegations of an affair with a *peruquier* and of hobnobbing with gypsies out of the window. . . .
(3) *The travels of Cosmo III . . . through England in the Reign of Charles II.* Translated (anonymously) from 'two immense folios' in the Laurentian Library, Florence, and printed in London for J. Mawman, 1821. There ought to be a new edition.
(4) Compare Chap. VI, n. 7
(5) Pl. 2973: 369, 370.
(6) *Diary*, November 13 1695.
(7) Bernard Lens was a member of a Flemish family of painters and engravers, one branch of whom established themselves in London in the late seventeenth century.
(8) For the *Wentworth Papers*, see Chap. VI.
(9) Op. cit., vol. 4, p. 299.
(10) Information from Portman Family Settled Estates (through Mr Gordon Mackenzie).
(11) The *Survey* (vol. XXIX, p. 66n) conjectures that this may have been the Thomas Ackres who drew a plan of the garden at Wrest Park, Bedfordshire, for the Duke of Kent (No. 4).
(12) This term was used occasionally in the early days ('ye above-mentioned Commissioners or Trustees' – Minute of July 17 1726).
(13) Just built (it will be remembered) on the site of the old Halifax House on the West side of the Square.
(14) The *Survey* quotes, among others, J. Ralph, *A Critical View of the Publick Buildings . . . in and around London* (1734), John Gwynn, *London and Westminster Improved* (1766) and even *The Builder*, as late as 1851.
(15) Vol. VI, by W. Weir, p. 200.

Chapter IV A Basin and a Statue

(1) The term applied to the very early type of steam engine associated with the name of Thomas Newcomen (1663–1729). Just when York Buildings installed theirs is not clear, but they had abandoned it by 1731. Dr Desagulier, a sort of technician-of-all-work to the Duke, seems to have experimented with 'fire engines' both at Marylebone and Cannons.
(2) Bridgeman in his estimate mentions 6 ft, but recent excavations have confirmed the lesser figure.
(3) Like so many of Chandos's speculations, York Buildings proved a financial quagmire. The New Company, formed in 1719, went into property, with ruinous results. A doggerel of the time says it all:

> You that are blessed with wealth by your Creator
> And want to drown your money in Thames water,
> Buy but York Buildings and the cistern there
> Will sink more pence than any fool can spare.

(4) Op. cit., vol. IV, p. 316.
(5) At No. 7 (1678–93) and No. 13 (1694).
(6) J. P. Malcolm, *Londinium Redivivum* (1802–7), vol. IV, p. 326.
(7) Illustrated in Gunnis, *Dictionary of British Sculptors*, pl. VIII.

(8) MS 13,910. The Archives include a mass of documentation relating to Samuel Travers's very remarkable will. In addition to providing for the statue, he left money to buy a George badge for the future Duke of Cumberland, in the event of his becoming a Knight of the Garter, and for annuities for additional Poor Knights of Windsor; the residue (which by 1804 appears to have reached the substantial sum of over £40,000) to be applied by Christ's Hospital to founding a Mathematical School for the sons of naval officers.
(9) Op. cit., p. 32.
(10) *Survey*, vol. XXIX, p. 69.
(11) *Foursome in St James's* (op. cit.), p. 45.

Chapter V The Architects Move In

(1) Still to be seen there, joined by the bridge from which Epstein's Madonna and Child are suspended in majesty.
(2) The *Survey*, on the whole, favours the claims of Edward Shepherd (builder of Shepherd Market), with perhaps some intervention by the Duke himself.
(3) *Georgian London* (London, Pleiades Books, 1945), p. 64.
(4) Robert Adam had already rebuilt No. 33, though in subdued and orthodox St James's Square brick.
(5) Quoted by the *Survey* from a Nostell Priory sale catalogue of 1916.
(6) His masterpiece was the second Newgate Gaol, demolished in 1902.
(7) Op. cit., pp. 125–6.
(8) Christopher Simon Sykes, op. cit., p. 207.
(9) In all, the Wyatt alterations cost the sizeable sum of nearly £28,000. The detailed bills survive, some of them being printed in Nigel Wratten's monograph, *The History and Architecture of No. 15 St James's Square* (produced for the Society).
(10) An imitation, rather than an exact copy, in plaster, of the famous original by Rysbrack at Chiswick House; it is probably contemporary.
(11) The Guinness interest in No. 11 (along with No. 12) came to an end in 1979. Both freeholds have recently been acquired by the property company MEPC.

Chapter VI A Study in Contrasts

(1) *The Wentworth Papers*, ed. J. J. Cartwright, 1883. The reference to 'Fubs' is on p. 64; to Old St Albans House on pp. 64–5.
(2) The Earldom of Strafford was not revived in his favour until 1711.
(3) Diary of John Hervey, 1st Earl of Bristol (Wells, E. Jackson, 1894), p. 55
(4) *The Wentworth Papers*, op. cit., p. 279 *et seq.*
(5) *Correspondence*, vol. 1, p. 285.
(6) Mark Girouard, *Life in the English Country House* (Yale 1978, Penguin 1980), pp. 147–8.
(7) They did themselves remarkably well, though – 60 meat dishes and 41 desserts, according to Swift.
(8) *The Norfolk House Music Room* (Victoria & Albert Museum, 1973). Among much else Mr Fitzgerald quotes a richly rewarding description of the house and the inaugural party by William Farington, brother of the famous diarist, and this reappears in *Private Palaces*, op. cit., pp. 130–38.
(9) Op. cit., pp. 197–8.
(10) Quoted in Fitzgerald, op. cit., p. 49.
(11) *The Creevey Papers*, ed. Sir Herbert Maxwell (1903).
(12) Born 1908, succeeded 1917. Subsequently a highly regarded Earl Marshal. Died 1975. Mr J. M. Robinson tells us that for years the Duke's father, that great Catholic layman, could not speak clearly, as the result of being hit in the mouth with a stone while playing with other children in the Square garden. (*The Dukes of Norfolk*, Oxford University Press, 1982, p. 214.)
(13) Submitted to the LCC's Planning and Building Regulation (London Development Sub-)Committee, December 7 1937.
(14) February 10, 1938, p. 15.
(15) *London: The Cities of London and Westminster*, op. cit., p. 568.
(16) By the mother's side. He took the name Brettingham as being likely to improve his professional prospects.
(17) Princess Lieven has given us a famous description of the bed proudly displayed in No. 21 by Lady Stewart; it was adorned with a baron's coronet 'the size of the crown of the King of Wurtemburg' and held up at the four corners by 'four large gilt figures of Hercules, nude and fashioned exactly like real men'. The bed figured again as an altar, as a sideboard and finally as a bed again at the christening of Lady Stewart's child. (*Private Letters of Princess Lieven* ed. Peter Quennell (John Murray, 1937), pp. 167, 171.)
(18) Fragments have recently been made more visible in Clink St, Bankside.
(19) There has always been some doubt whether she was so in the strictly physical sense. The relationship was predominantly domestic on his side, mercenary on hers.
(20) George Henry Sumner, *Life of Charles Richard Sumner D.D.* (London, John Murray, 1876), p. 19 *et seq.*
(21) The story is strongly controverted by A. Aspinall, *Letters of King George IV* (Cambridge, 1938), vol. II, p. 425 *et seq.*
(22) Op. cit. (above), p. 147.
(23) 'Full membership, Gentlemen £10.10*s.*; Ladies £3.3*s.*; Dance Section £3.3*s.*', according to an advertisement of August 1925. But a reference to 'Forty Bedrooms Available' suggests that the Bishops of Winchester must have had even more houseroom than their brethren of London across the Square.

Chapter VII Disturbers of the Peace

(1) *London Journal*, August 19 1727, quoted by Dasent.
(2) *Last Journals* (John Lane, 1910), vol. 1, p. 238.

(3) *Journal*, vol. IV, p. 106. ''Tis terrible,' Lady Mary comments elsewhere, 'the number of servants who have taken to that Profession', and she cites a robbery carried out by a former coachman to Lord Palmerston [No. 3].
(4) See FC6 in the Arundel Castle Archives.
(5) Robert Villiers, 3rd Viscount Purbeck, was so styled although, because of some doubt about his father's legitimacy, he never received a Writ of Summons to the House of Lords. His duelling propensities brought him to his death at Liége in 1684, still under 30 years of age.
(6) *Journal to Stella*, Letter LV, Nov. 15 1712.
(7) *The History of Henry Esmond* (Book 3), 1852.
(8) The Protestant mobsters resented his sponsorship of the Catholic Relief Bill of 1778.
(9) *Select Views of London* (1816), p. 34.
(10) *Reminiscences of Captain Gronow* (London, Nimmo, 1900), vol. I, p. 220. Walford, *Old and New London*, 1872–78, vol. IV, p. 190) alleges that a blunderbuss was fired from the window of No. 18 which 'proved fatal to two innocent persons'. One wonders, incidentally, whether Gronow confused the Bishop of London's house with the Bishop of Winchester's, only three doors away from No. 18.
(11) Rush was Minister in London from 1817 to 1825. His *A Residence at the Court of London* was published in 1833.

Chapter VIII From Gravell'd Walk to Garden

(1) For example, their treatment of the Palladian design put forward by Lord Burlington for the proposed Mansion House. The first question asked in Court, Stuart assures us, was whether 'this Palladio' was a Freeman of the City. When it became clear that he was no such thing – and a Papist to boot – the job was handed to a Freeman and a Protestant 'who had originally been a shipwright' (the elder George Dance).
(2) The sequence of events is well set out in *Survey*, vol. XXIX, pp. 352–4. The lighting schemes in Piccadilly etc. were carried out by the Vestry of St James's; the Square of course was a private enterprise affair.
(3) At that period the eldest son and heir of the Duke of Norfolk was known as the Earl of Surrey.
(4) Knight's *London*, vol. VI, p. 200.

Chapter IX The 'Other' No. 10

(1) The term 'medallion' would perhaps exclude the rectangular inscription which records the World War II rôle of Norfolk House (p. 136).
(2) This chapter owes much to *Chatham House and its Neighbours* (1959), compiled by C. E. Carrington for the Institute of International Affairs.

Chapter X Commerce Rears Its Head

(1) Barbara and Hensleigh Wedgwood, *The Wedgwood Circle*, 1730–1897 (London, Studio Vista, 1980), where much of the data about the Wedgwoods in St James's Square (or 'York St', as they preferred to call it) was brought together for the first time. See also *Foursome in St James's* (op. cit., chap. 8) for the story of No. 8 as the Sports Club as well as Wedgwood headquarters.
(2) *National Westminster Bank; St James's Square 1834–1984* (published by the Bank).
(3) In the archives of the Clerical, Medical and General Life Assurance Society.
(4) Published by the Society in 1924. Besant was General Manager and Actuary at the time.
(5) A copy of this very interesting document survives in the archives of No. 15.

Chapter XI . . . And then the Clubs

(1) For Scrope Davies as gambler, politician and above all as friend of Byron, see T. A. J. Burnett, *The Rise and Fall of a Dandy* (London, John Murray, 1981), based largely on the remarkable discovery of a trunk-load of his papers in a bank vault in 1976.
(2) . . . when your mind's made up to go
To-night to Mrs Boehm's masquerade,
Spectator, or partaker, of the show . . .
— *Beppo* (1817), LVI

According to Augustus Hare (*Walks in London*, 1883, vol. II, p. 56), the play presented by Lord Hardwicke's family and friends at No. 3 was Racine's *Mithridate*; he tells us that Byron was 'of the company', but whether as performer or auditor is not clear.
(3) Journal entry for November 28 1813 in vol. 3 of *Byron's Letters and Journals*, ed. L. H. Marchand (Murray, 1974). We do not know exactly at which number in the Square this famous dinner party took place. For many years the Hollands wintered in central London, using Holland House, Kensington, as a summer residence only. They are known to have rented No. 10 in about 1813–14 and 'No. 21a' in 1819, and to have been sub-tenants of the Duke of Bedford at No. 15 in 1823 and 1826.
(4) E. C. Mayne, *Life and Letters of Anne Isabella, Lady Noel Byron* (Constable, 1929), pp. 301–2.
(5) *Chatham House and its Neighbours*, op. cit., pp. 22–4.
(6) 1st Northumberland (1699–1708), 8th Norfolk (1720–22), 3rd Beaufort (1730–33), 3rd, 4th and 5th Roxburgh (1796–1812), 4th Portland (1819–26), 4th and 5th Atholl (1827–30, 1834–35).
(7) Subsequently it united with the Orleans and the Marlborough to form the Marlborough-Windham, but this in turn folded.
(8) See Chap. X, n. 1
(9) The house was then owned by Burrage Angier (see p. 5) and his daughter.

(10) For a fuller account of the Boehms at No. 16 and the events of June 21, see *Foursome in St James's*, op. cit., pp. 13–15. Wellington's Dispatch itself emphasized the casualties.
(11) For over a hundred years from its construction in 1726 (p. 39), No. 17 had been occupied by only two families, the Bridgmans (1726–89) and Sir Philip Francis, his widow and his son (1790–1837). Thereafter a club (the Colonial) briefly appeared, but in 1839 Mr John Howell of West Wickham, Kent, bought out the Francis interest and converted No. 17 into 'club chambers'. It was therefore ripe for an East India Club takeover by 1863.
(12) Short for 'Rag and Famish'. This was the nickname of a low dive in Cranborne Alley and was conferred jocosely upon the club by a certain Capt. W. H. Duff round about 1839. At least that is the tale as told by the club's historian, Capt. C. W. Firebrace, in Chap. I of *The Army and Navy Club 1837–1933* (John Murray, 1934), but it does not explain the origins of the phrase itself.
(13) The *Survey of London* itself includes the Rag in its St James's Square rather than its Pall Mall section, perhaps on the strength of its having absorbed the site of one undoubted Square house '21a'.
(14) Under the patronage, it seems, of Lord Iveagh next door. He is said to have added the freehold of No. 12 to that of No. 11 in order to ease the club's financial worries.
(15) Ed. Miron Grindea (Boydell Press, 1978).
(16) Its armchairs can also induce sleep. A friend of the writer used to allege that having sunk into one of them after a too hospitable luncheon, he woke up to find himself on the 'platform' of the AGM, with T. S. Eliot on one side of him and Dame Edith Sitwell on the other. Typical 'LL' apocrypha.
(17) Following the Rating and Valuation (Miscellaneous Provisions) Act, 1955, Westminster City Council levied rates on the Library, which had hitherto been exempt under the Scientific and Literary Societies Act of 1843. When the Library registered as a charity in 1969, its rates were reduced by 50 per cent; even so they have increased from just under £5000 in 1956 to over £20,000 in 1986.

Chapter XII Victorian Heyday

(1) *The Francis Letters*, ed. Beata Francis & Eliza Keary (Hutchinson, 1901), Vol. II, p. 567.
(2) This would be Bishop Beilby Porteous (No. 33, 1788–1809); for the eccentricities of the 11th Duke of Norfolk, see p. 67.
(3) The fact that the sole record of this incident is to be found not in the Minutes of the St James's Square Trust but in those of the East India Club Committee (see *Foursome in St James's*, op. cit. p. 47), is a reminder how limited our sources are, in the absence of correspondence which would put flesh on the bare bones of the Trustees' annual proceedings.
(4) *Foursome in St James's*, op. cit., pp. 45–6.
(5) Op. cit., p. 196.
(6) Op. cit., pp. 57–60.
(7) D. M. Forrest, *The Oriental* (Rev. edn, 1979), p. 179 *et seq.*
(8) R. E. Balfour, *A Short History of Hawker Siddeley House* (for the Hawker Siddeley Group, 1949), pp. 11–12.
(9) After the death of Algernon Capel, 2nd Earl of Essex in 1692, it had become the property of the West Country family of Popham, and was rented for a time by the 8th Duke of Norfolk and the Venetian Ambassador, Signor Tron.
(10) *The Complete Peerage*, ed. Hon. Vicary Gibbs (Norwich, St Catherine's Press), Vol. III, article CLEVELAND.
(11) *Creevey Papers*, op. cit., p. 428.
(12) *The London Library*, op. cit., p. 23.
(13) *Foursome in St James's*, op. cit., p. 10n.

Chapter XIII Towards the Brink

(1) Among its earlier manifestations were the rescue of two members from a prison van in Manchester in July 1867 (followed by five death sentences, three of which were carried out), and the explosion of a powder barrel against the wall of Clerkenwell Gaol later in the same year.
(2) *Life and Letters of Mandell Creighton*, by his wife (Longmans, 1904), p. 225.
(3) S. C. Carpenter, *Winnington-Ingram* (Hodder & Stoughton, 1949), p. 88 *et seq.* The late Paul Paget, architect son of Winnington-Ingram's old friend and Suffragan, Bishop Luke Paget, remembered staying at No. 32 as a very small boy and watching the revolving globe on the Coliseum out of a top back window. Surprisingly, this object dates from about 1904.
(4) Intricate descents in the female line from Henry, Duke of Kent (p. 46) brought de Greys and Granthams to No. 4 in the eighteenth/nineteenth centuries. Anne Florence, daughter and heiress of the 3rd Earl de Grey, was born in the Square and died there in 1880, having lived a grand social life as wife of the 6th Earl Cowper. Her son Francis, the 7th Earl, died childless and was succeeded by his nephew Auberon Herbert, 8th Baron Lucas and 11th Dingwall, the beloved 'Bron' of the Belloc/Baring circle before World War I. He sold No. 4 to the Astors and was killed serving with the Royal Flying Corps in November 1916.
(5) For the connection of the same family with No. 9, see p. 107.
(6) Thanks are due to Verily Anderson for permission to quote from her *The Northrepps Grandchildren* (Hodder & Stoughton, 1968), and for private information.
(7) Alastair Service, *Edwardian Architecture* (London, Thames & Hudson, 1977), p. 186.
(8) For Lutyens in Apple Tree Yard, see Christopher Hussey, *The Life of Sir Edwin Lutyens* (London, Country Life, 1950), p. 294; for Nicholson see Marguerite Steen's enchanting biography, *William*

Nicholson (London, Collins, 1943), p. 126 *et seq.* According to Miss Steen, No. 11 was a 'derelict half-broken-down stable' when Nicholson took it over.
(9) *London's Open-air Statuary* (London, Longmans Green, 1928), pp. 16–18.
(10) British Architectural Library, Lutyens Collection.
(11) Rental £1200 for a term of 21 years. The lease goes into considerable detail about the care and insurance of the precious furniture, fittings and pictures. Even ceiling mouldings are specified, but the highest individual value is £1000 for 'a pair of Adams richly carved gilt console tables painted with mythological subjects'. The big oil painting on the stairs, 'the Ascension after Raffaelle' (see also p. 47) is to be insured for a modest £100.

Chapter XIV Butlers, Bombs and Ernest Bevin

(1) *The Pretty Lady* (London, Cassell, 1918), pp. 50–51.
(2) Piers Brendon, *Head of Guinness* (Privately printed, 1979), p. 92.
(3) Arundel Castle Archives A76.
(4) *Private Palaces* (op. cit.), p. 168.
(5) Referring no doubt to the 'dog-leg' through which the service quarters extended towards Charles II St.
(6) This somehow takes one back to the days when the Duke of Chandos used to have supplies sent up three days a week from Canons in a vast *chasse-marée* – bread in one box, meat in another, linen in a third, appropriate officials keeping the keys of each compartment – and his letters were carried by a boy on a little Welsh pony, 'such as run upon the hills'.
(7) *Private Palaces* (op. cit.), p. 326.
(8) Cmd. Paper 3196 (HM Stationery Office, 1928).
(9) May 3 1923.
(10) *Report of the Working Party on Car Parking in the Inner Area of London.* HMSO, 1953.
(11) Two surface shelters were in fact erected at a cost of £2,650 and there were additional public shelters in the basements of No. 3, No. 8 and perhaps other houses. See Minutes of Westminster City Council Emergency and Civil Defence (Special) Committees, 1939 *et. seq.*
(12) For this and other movements at the time, see *Foursome in St James's*, op. cit., p. 133 *et seq.*
(13) James Lees-Milne, *Another Self* (London, Hamish Hamilton, 1970), p. 151.
(14) Information from Parks, Palaces and Central Services Secretariat, Ministry of the Environment. Rupert Gunnis is incorrect in stating in his *Dictionary of British Sculptors* (p. 446) that Mathew Wyatt's George III in Cockspur St was one of only two statues that went to the country.
(15) Government departments were still in No. 33, on a rental basis, for some time longer.

Chapter XV A Last Look Round

(1) Between 1947 and 1976, Norfolk House was the headquarters of British Aluminium. The present tenants are Lamco Paper Sales Ltd and allied companies. Their neighbours at No. 32 are Goddard Kay Rogers and Associates.
(2) Now D'Arcy Masius Benton & Bowles.
(3) Mr Wallace's earlier allies included representatives of the Guinness Trustees (Nos. 11/12) and the Army & Navy Club, with the Distillers' interests (Nos. 20/21) joining in soon afterwards. Guinness and Distillers were generous contributors to the restoration fund.
(4) In spite of this intrusive plural, the 'garden' has always been referred to as such since its creation.
(5) Apparently the marble group of 'Venus and Cupid' presented to the Club in 1934 by Lord Stanhope. A deputation consisting of Messrs Noel-Smith (London Library) and Ian Grey (Chatham House) reported that though it had merits, it was 'entirely unsuitable' for St James's Square.
(6) Letter from Miss Rosemarie Peters. In addition to the species she lists, a few years ago a duck succeeded in raising her brood in the shrubberies, and kestrels have been seen hovering when the garden is closed, which suggests mice and voles among the fauna. On the other hand a grass snake which made a sensational appearance was probably 'planted'; ditto a handsome cock pheasant.
(7) Property 'arm' of The Distillers Company plc.
(8) The history of this building had been somewhat intricate since Lord Derby sold out to English Law Life Assurance in 1912. It was later occupied in part by commercial firms (including Lord Leverhulme's MacFisheries enterprise) and in part by the Caledonian Club, which in 1931 combined its upper storeys with No. 32, while the National Provincial Bank moved into the ground floor. After the club and the bank had been bombed out, a long spell of Government occupation followed, only ended by the Hammerson takeover.
(9) Correspondence in *The Times*, January 5–11 1971.

Sources

The structure of this book can be said to have a triangular foundation, two elements of which have already been indicated in the Foreword by the Chairman of the St James's Square Trustees. They are the Minute Books of the Trust itself and Arthur Irwin Dasent's *History* (1895). While the Minute Books are of course invaluable, going back as they do to the very creation of the Trust, individual entries are on the whole disappointingly terse, and there is virtually no correspondence in support until quite recent times. The earliest Minute Book (now lodged at the City of Westminster's Local History Library) runs from 1726 to 1835; its successor (in the keeping of the Trust) from that year until the present day. There is also a useful Trustees' Rate Book, showing annual contributions by owners or tenants from 1845 onwards.

As for Dasent, every explorer of the Square's past must be grateful for the exemplary spadework he did in extracting (mainly from the Parish of St James's own Rate Books) the occupancies of each individual house, from seventeenth-century beginnings until his *History* was published by Macmillan in 1895. Moreover, he takes the trouble to list Parish (as distinct from Square) Rates being paid at ten-year intervals. His text is almost equally informative, even though he diversifies now and then into a sort of documentary fiction – 'A Day in the Life of Charles II' or 'One Hundred Years Ago' (a corresponding ramble round the Square by the Prince Regent).

The third stout prop on which reliance has been placed throughout is *The Survey of London*, conducted over a long period under the auspices of the former London County Council. Two volumes, XXIX and XXX (published by the Athlone Press in 1960), are devoted to the Parish of St James Westminster (south of Piccadilly). Five chapters in the former cover, with meticulous scholarship, the Bailiwick of St James, the Parish and Vestry, the Church and finally the Square itself and its individual houses; Vol. XXX backs them up with sixteen pages of references and seventy-four beautifully reproduced plates. The use which has been made of all this, with the generous co-operation of the Survey, goes far beyond the specific references footnoted from time to time.

More limited in scope of course, but often valuable, are the various monographs and booklets in which firms or institutions have recorded information about the historic houses which they occupy; these too have been footnoted but, being privately produced, have not been included in the bibliographical summary below. Nor has it been thought necessary to list such immortal standbys as the Diaries of Samuel Pepys and John Evelyn, or the inexhaustible Journals and Correspondence of Horace Walpole.

Works Consulted

ANDERSON, VERILY, *The Northrepps Grandchildren*, London, 1929.
ANON. (James Stuart?), *Critical Observations on the Buildings and Improvements of London*, London, 1771.
ASPINALL, A., *Letters of King George IV*, Cambridge, 1938.
BOSWELL, JAMES, *Life of Samuel Johnson*, various editions.
BURNETT, T. A. J., *The Rise and Fall of a Dandy* [Scrope Davies], London, 1981.
BYRON, LORD, *Letters and Journals*, ed. Marchant, London, 1974.
CARPENTER, S. C., *Winnington-Ingram*, London, 1929.
CARTE, THOMAS, *Life of James Butler, 1st Duke of Ormonde*, Oxford, 1836.
CATHCART, HELEN, *The Queen Mother Herself*, London, 1979.

CHANCELLOR, BERESFORD, *History of the Squares of London*, London, 1905; *Private Palaces of London*, London, 1908.
COKE, LADY MARY, *Journals*, London (reprinted), Bath 1970.
CREEVEY, THOMAS, *The Creevey Papers*, ed. Sir H. Maxwell, London, 1903.
CREIGHTON, LOUISE, *Life and Letters of Mandell Creighton*, London, 1904.
FIREBRACE, Capt. C. W., *The Army and Navy Club*, London, 1934.
FITZGERALD, DESMOND, *The Norfolk House Music Room*, London, 1973.
FORREST, D. M., *The Oriental*, rev. ed. London, 1979; *Foursome in St James's*, London, 1982.
FRANCIS, BEATA, and KEARY, ELIZA, *The Francis Letters*, London, 1901.
GIBBS, Hon. VICARY, *The Complete Peerage*, new edn. 1910, *et seq.*
GIROUARD, MARK, *Life in the English Country House*, Yale, 1978, London, 1980.
GLEICHEN, LORD EDWARD, *London's Open-Air Statuary*, London, 1928.
GRONOW, Capt. R. H., *Reminiscences*, London, 1900.
GUNNIS, R., *Dictionary of British Sculptors*, London, 1951.
GWYNN, J., *London and Westminster Improved*, London, 1766.
HARE, AUGUSTUS, *Walks About London*, London, 1883.
HERVEY, JOHN, 1st Earl of Bristol, *Diary* and *Letter Books*, ed. Jackson, Wells, 1894.
HUSSEY, CHRISTOPHER, *Life of Sir Edwin Lutyens*, London, 1950.
KNIGHT, CHARLES, *London*, London, 1841, *et seq.*
LEES-MILNE, JAMES, *Another Self*, London, 1970; *Prophesying Peace*, London, 1977.
LIEVEN, PRINCESS, *private letters*, ed. Peter Quennell, London, 1937.
LUTTRELL, NARCISSUS, *Brief Historical Relation of State Affairs*, reprinted Oxford, 1857.
MAGALOTTI, LORENZO, *The Travels of Cosmo II . . . through England in the Reign of Charles II*, London, 1821.
MALCOLM, J. P., *Londinium Redivivum*, London, 1802–7.
OMAN, CAROLA, *Henrietta Maria*, London, 1936.
PAPWORTH, J. P., *Select Views of London*, London, 1816.
PENNANT, T., *Some Account of London*, London, 1793.
PEVSNER, NIKOLAUS, *London, The Cities of London & Westminster*, London, 1957.
RALPH, J. *A Critical View of the Public Buildings in and around London*, London, 1734.
RERESBY, Sir JOHN, *Memoirs*, ed. A. Browning, Glasgow, 1931.
ROBINSON, J. M., *The Dukes of Norfolk*, Oxford, 1982.
ROBINSON, J. R., *The Princely Chandos*, London, 1893.
RUSH, W. A., *A Residence at the Court of London*, 1833.
ST HELIER, Lady, *Memoirs of Fifty Years*, London, 1901.
SERVICE, ALISTAIR, *Edwardian Architecture*, London, 1977.
SEYMOUR, R. *A Survey of the Cities of London & Westminster*, London, 1735.
SUMMERSON, JOHN, *Georgian London*, London, 1945.
SUMNER, G. H., *Life of Charles Richard Sumner*, London, 1876.
SWIFT, JONATHAN, *Correspondence* and *Journal to Stella* (various editions).
SYKES, C. S., *Private Palaces*, London, 1985.
WALFORD, EDWARD, *Old and New London*, London, 1872–78.
WEDGWOOD, B. & H., *The Wedgwood Circle*, London, 1980.
Wentworth Papers, ed. J. J. Cartright, London, 1883.
WHEATLEY, H. B., *About Piccadilly and Pall-Mall*, 1870.

Appendix I
Trustees of St James's Square – 1986

Geoffrey Evett	National Westminster Bank plc (No. 1)
Graham Gent	D'Arcy Masius Benton & Bowles (No. 2)
David Greer	James Buchanan & Co. Ltd (No. 3)
Terry Ball	RTZ Services Ltd (No. 6)
Richard Coleman	Royal Fine Arts Commission (No. 7)
Gordon Perry	ENSERCH House Inc. (No. 8)
Derek Williams	Charterhall plc (No. 8)
Miss Eileen Menzies	Royal Institute of International Affairs (No. 10)
Barry Vardill	MEPC plc (Nos. 11/12)
David Brooks	Grindlays Bank Ltd. (No. 13)
Douglas Matthews	The London Library (No. 14)
Bernard High	Clerical, Medical & General Life Assurance Society (No. 15)
John Stoy	The East India Club (Nos. 16/17)
Phil Hyson	Hawker Siddeley Group Ltd (No. 18)
Henry Arnott	Prudential Assurance Co. Ltd (No. 19)
Dennis Hill (Chairman)	Winchester House Property Co. Ltd (Nos. 20/21)
Denis O'Reilly	Army & Navy Club (No. 22)
Roger Longley*	Chem Systems International Ltd (No. 28)
Kevin Hodges	Lamco Paper Sales Ltd (No. 31)
Roy Goddard	Goddard Kay Rogers & Associates (No. 32)
Mrs Gisela Gledhill	Consolidated Gold Fields plc (No. 33)

* Co-opted, representing South side.

Appendix Ia

Trustees of St James's Square - 2001

Anders Wensfelt	Ericsson	Nos. 1 & 2
Graham Stanton	John D Wood	No. 3
Michael Ebbitt	Naval & Military Club	No. 4
Paul Owen	Rio Tinto	Nos. 5 & 6
Geoffrey King	Slater, Chapman & Cooke	No. 7
Tim Bowen	Universal Music International Ltd	No 8
Dawn Margrett	Royal Institute of International Affairs	Nos. 9 & 10
To be appointed	Regus Conference Limited	Nos. 11 & 12
To be appointed	U.K.I	No. 13
Trevor Elliott	The London Library	No. 14
Charles Hunter	Clerical Medical Investment	No. 15
Michael Howell (Deputy Chairman)	East India Club	Nos. 16 & 17
Stephen Gayer	Hamptons International	No. 18
Tim Cameron Jones	CB Hillier Parker	No. 19
Jeff Hobson	CB Hillier Parker	Nos. 20 & 21
Anthony Holt	Army & Navy Club	No. 36 Pall Mall with frontage onto St James's Square
John Morris	Russell Reynolds	No. 24
Kevin Hodges	UPM-Kymmere Ltd	No. 31
Peter Alcock	Williams Holdings Plc	No. 32
Ron Adam	HQ Executive Offices (UK) Ltd	No. 33
John Stevens (Chairman)		
Dennis Hill (President)		

Appendix II
The Square, House by House

HOUSE	BUILDERS/DEVELOPERS	NOTABLE OWNERS/OCCUPIERS	CURRENT OWNERSHIP/ OCCUPANCY
No. 1 (part of Ossulston House 1677–1752)	1677 1st Lord Arlington	1677–1752 Bennet family (Arlington, Ossulston, Tankerville)	
	1752 rebuilt as No. 1	1756–1844 Legge family, Earls of Dartmouth	
		(1806–30 rented by 3rd Baron Grantham)	Freeholders: National Westminster Bank plc
	1940 bomb damage		
	1956–8 rebuilt (Mewès & Davis)	1844– London & Westminster (now National Westminster) Bank	Part tenants: Messrs D'Arcy Masius Benton & Bowles
No. 2 (part of Ossulston House 1677–1752, as above)		1677–1752 (as Ossulston House above)	
	1752 rebuilt as No. 2	1754–1923 Boscawen family, Viscounts Falmouth	
	1940 demolished (bombing)	1923–44 Canada Life Assurance	Freeholders: National Westminster Bank plc
	1956–58 rebuilt with No. 1 (as above)		Tenants: Messrs D'Arcy Masius Benton & Bowles
No. 3 (Buchanan House)	1675 Edward Shaw (builder)	1675–1710 (short lets intervening) William Cavendish (later 1st Duke of Devonshire)	
	1712–14 rebuilt (? Nicholas Hawksmoor)	1710–16 3rd Baron (later 1st Earl) Ashburnham	Freeholders: Clerical, Medical & General Life Assurance Society (since 1936)
		1717–59 1st and 2nd Viscounts Palmerston	
		1763–99 5th Earl (later 1st Marquess) of Donegal	Tenants: James Buchanan & Co. Ltd The Laird Group plc M.E.D.P. Delta Group Ltd Al Mal International Ltd The Attock Oil Co. Ltd T.W.O. (UK) Ltd Jardine Investment Management Ltd
		1801–34 3rd Earl of Hardwicke	
		1839–52 S. W. Lane Fox MP	
		1854–1922 Copyhold, Enclosure and Tithe Commission	
	1934 rebuilt (Messrs A. & D. Ospalek) as flats – never used as such	1923 onwards misc. offices	
No. 4	1676 Nicholas Barbon	1677–1702 10th Earl of Kent	
	1725 rebuilt after fire (? Edward Shepherd)	1703–40 11th Earl and 1st Duke	
		1744–90 2nd Earl of Hardwicke; 1791–97 his widow Jemima Marchioness de Grey; 1798–1833, his daughter Amabel, Countess de Grey	
		1834–59 Earl de Grey	
		1860–80, Anne Florence Countess Cowper; 1884–1905, 7th Earl Cowper	
		1912–42 2nd Viscount Astor	
		1943–45 (under requisition), Free French Forces etc.	
		1947–68 Arts Council of Great Britain	
		1971– Crown Court, then Employment Appeal Tribunal	H.M. Government

HOUSE	BUILDERS/DEVELOPERS	NOTABLE OWNERS/OCCUPIERS	CURRENT OWNERSHIP/ OCCUPANCY
No. 5	1675 George Clisby 1748–49 rebuilt (Matthew Brettingham senr) 1854 refacing and additional storey (Messrs Cubitt)	1680–91 Countess of Thanet 1711–1973 Wentworth/Byng family, Earls of Strafford	Libyan People's Bureau
No. 6	1673–76 Abraham Story 1819–20 rebuilt (John Field) 1958 rebuilt (Fitzroy Robinson & Partners)	1677–1955 Hervey family, Earls and later Marquesses of Bristol 1955–60 Lady Elizabeth Byng 1961 leased by Consolidated Zinc Corp.; 1975 freehold bought by RTZ	RTZ Ltd
No. 7	1674 John Angier	1678–93 1st Earl of Ranelagh 1694–1723 2nd Earl of Radnor 1724–69 Scawen family (1744–60, let) 1770–81 1st and 2nd Earls of Warwick 1797–1909 Egerton family (later Barons and Earls Egerton of Tatton)	
	1911 rebuilt (Sir Edwin Lutyens)	1909–43 Gaspard, William and Henry Farrer 1943–82 under requisition, then lease, for Ministry of Labour and National Service	Freeholders: Property Service Agency (for Royal Fine Arts Commission and Museums and Galleries Commission)
No. 8 (Enserch House)	1676 St Albans family	1676 (and later) French Ambassador 1689–1721 St Albans family (with lettings) 1721–49 Sir Mathew Decker and widow 1722–84 Sir Sampson Gideon Bt 1796–1830 Josiah Wedgwood jnr 1831–39 2nd Earl of Romney 1855–76 Charity Commissioners 1879–88 Clubs (various) 1893–1938 Sports Club	
	1939 rebuilt (Angel & Curtis)	1943–80 under requisition, then lease Ministry of Labour & Nat. Service	Freeholders: PosTel Investments Tenants: ENSERCH House Inc.
Nos. 9–11 (as one house)	1677 1st Earl of St Albans	1677–82 1st Earl of St Albans 1682–1719 1st and 2nd Dukes of Ormonde; Earl of Arran	
	1735–36 demolished	1719–35 1st Duke of Chandos	
No. 9	1736 Henry Flitcroft (Benjamin Timbrell, builder)	1736–59 Wollaston family 1790–1887 Hoare family (ending with Mrs Anne Hoare, aged 100) 1888–1943 Portland Club	Royal Institute of International Affairs

HOUSE	BUILDERS/DEVELOPERS	NOTABLE OWNERS/OCCUPIERS	CURRENT OWNERSHIP/ OCCUPANCY
No. 10	(as above)	1736–1890 Heathcote family, Baronets *let to* 1759–62 1st Earl of Chatham 1820–29 2nd Earl of Blessington 1837–54 14th Earl of Derby 1855–89 1st Baron Tollemache 1890 Rt Hon. W. E. Gladstone 1890–1923 1st Baron Kinnaird	(as No. 9 above)
No. 11	(as above)	1737–64 2nd Earl of Macclesfield 1767–85 Sir Rowland Winn, 5th Bt 1798–1817 Alexander Davison 1823–64 Hudson Gurney 1876–98 Sir Joseph Bailey, 1st Bt 1905–79 Hon. Rupert Guinness (later 2nd Earl of Iveagh), followed by other members of the Guinness family and Iveagh Trustees 1979–86 Freeholders: Imperial Group *c.* 1969–86 Tenants: Property Services Agency (for Arbitration and Conciliation Service ACAS)	Freeholders: MEPC plc Tenants: ACAS
No. 12	1674 Sir Cyril Wyche 1836 rebuilt (Thomas Cubitt)	1686–1733 8th Earl of Pembroke, and widow (1755–58, 10th Earl) 1803–32 Wedderburn/Erskine family, Earls of Rosslyn 1835–45 8th Lord King (later Earl of Lovelace) 1859–79 7th Duke of Marlborough 1909–42 British Empire Club 1942–79 Earl of Iveagh and other Guinness interests (then as No. 11 above)	(as No. 11 above)
No. 13	1675 Sir Thomas Clarges (Clarges family freeholders about 60 years) 1735–37 rebuilt (Matthew Brettingham)	1676–1754 short tenancies (including 1695–98 Dutch Ambassador and 1723–25 the Admiralty) 1738–94 Sir Henry Liddell (later 1st Lord Ravensworth) and widow 1796–1812 3rd, 4th and 5th Dukes of Roxburgh 1836–1941 Windham Club 1944–53 Ministry of Labour and National Service (with No. 12)	Freeholders: Clerical, Medical & General Life Assurance Soc. (since 1977) Tenants: Grindlays Bank plc
No. 14	1673 Richard Frith	1676–78 Sir Fulke Lacy 1680–98 Williams family, of Thanet 1699–1704 Anne Lady Crewe	

HOUSE	BUILDERS/DEVELOPERS	NOTABLE OWNERS/OCCUPIERS	CURRENT OWNERSHIP/ OCCUPANCY
		1705–16 1st Earl of Torrington (married to the above)	
		1719–24 1st Earl of Portmore	
		1768–73 Sir Charles Asgill, 1st Bt (Lord Mayor of London)	
		1799–1845 1st Earl Beauchamp and his widow	
	1896–8 rebuilt (J. Osborne Smith)	1845 onwards, London Library	London Library
No. 15	1673 Richard Frith	1678–79 Frances, Duchess of Richmond	
		1687–1722 Marchioness de Gouvernet	
		1723–49 4th Earl of Clarendon	
	1763–66 rebuilt (James Stuart)	1766–1854 Anson family, later Earls of Lichfield (frequently let)	
		1856 onwards Clerical, Medical & General Life Assurance Soc.	Clerical, Medical & General Life Assurance Soc.
No. 16	1676 John Angier	1676–78 3rd Viscount Purbeck	
		1691–1704 1st Earl of Romney	
		1705–69 Sir John Germain 1st Bt and his widow (Lady Betty)	
	1790 demolished; 1807 rebuilt	1807–19 Edward Boehm	
		1826–43 1st Marquess of Clanricarde	
	1863 partly rebuilt with No. 17 (Charles Lee and Charles Fish)	1850 rented, then bought outright, East India United Service Club	East India, Devonshire, Sports and Public School Club
Nos. 17–18 (as Halifax House)	1673 1st Marquess of Halifax	1673–1707 1st and 2nd Marquesses of Halifax and latter's widow	
	1725 rebuilt as two houses (Thomas Phillips)	1708–19 1st Duke of Roxburgh	
No. 17		1726–89 Bridgman family, Earls of Bradford	
		1790–1837 Sir Philip Francis, his widow and son	
		(1820 let to Queen Caroline)	
		1843–62 John Howell (Club Chambers)	
	1863 rebuilt with No. 16 (as above)	1863 bought by East India United Service Club for extension	(as No. 16 above)
No. 18		1727–33 4th Earl of Chesterfield	
		1734–72 Sir John Heathcote, 2nd Bt, and his widow	
		1794–1803 1st Baron Thurlow	
		1806–29 2nd Marquess of Londonderry and his widow	
		1831–37 Oxford & Cambridge Club	
		1838–45 Army & Navy Club	
	1846–48 (Elger & Kelk)	1846–76 Sir John Kelk (thereafter Club Chambers and offices)	Hawker Siddeley Group (from 1944)

HOUSE	BUILDERS/DEVELOPERS	NOTABLE OWNERS/OCCUPIERS	CURRENT OWNERSHIP/ OCCUPANCY
No. 19	1674 Richard Frith	1677–86 Capel family, Earls of Essex	Freeholders: Prudential Assurance Co. (from 1966)
		1716–19 Venetian Ambassador	Tenants:
		1721–1891 Fitzroy/Vane family, Dukes of Cleveland	Hill Samuel & Co. Ltd Fischer Fine Art Ltd
	1897 rebuilt (Rolfe & Mathews)	(1897 onwards offices and residential)	Silks Restaurants (London) Ltd
	1965–68 rebuilt (Chapman, Taylor Partners)		Babcock International plc Colouthros (Chartering) Ltd St James's Venture Capital Fund Ltd RTZ Ltd
No. 20	c. 1674 Abraham Storey	1676–1771 Apsley/Bathurst family	
	1772–74 rebuilt (Robert Adam)		
		1775–1920 Williams Wynn family	
		(1906–20, let to 14th Earl of Strathmore & Kinghorne)	
		1920–35 Messrs Eagle, Star & British Dominion Insurance Co. and Messrs Hamptons	
	1936 joined to No. 21 (Mewès & Davis)	1935 onwards, The Distillers Co. plc	The Distillers Co. plc
No. 21	1673 Trustees of Arabella Churchill	1673–78 Arabella Churchill	
		1685–96 Countess of Dorchester	
		1711–17, 1724–39 Portmore family	
	1791 rebuilt (R. Brettingham)	1742–1802, 4th, 5th & 6th Dukes of Leeds	
		1807–16 Union Club	
		1818–28 8th and 9th Dukes of St Albans	
		1829–75 Bishops of Winchester	
	1923 proposed rebuilding for National Sporting Club	1877–1924 War Office and other Govt Depts	
	1935–36 rebuilt, joined to No. 20 (Mewès & Davis)	1923–26 Centaur Club	
		1936 onwards The Distillers Co. plc	(as No. 20 above)
No. '21a'	1673 Edward Shaw	1673–87 Mary Davis	
		1720–43 1st Earl of Wilmington	
		1751–71 Thomas Brand MP and Thomas Brand jnr	
		1781–95 Hon. Henry Drummond MP	
		1799–1817 Samuel Thornton	
	1847 demolished	1820–46 1st Lord de Mauley	
Army & Navy Club (partly on site of '21a')	1848 Parnell & Smith		
	1962 rebuilt (T. P. Bennett & Son)		Army & Navy Club
No. 31 (south portion)	1665 1st Earl of St Albans	1667–77 Earl of St Albans	
		1677–93 2nd Earl of Feversham	
		1694–1708 2nd and 3rd Earls of Sunderland	
	1713–14 'Old Norfolk House' built at rear	1710–22 1st Duke of Portland	
		1722–47 8th and 9th Dukes of Norfolk	
	1748 demolished	(let 1738–41 to George Prince of Wales)	

HOUSE	BUILDERS/DEVELOPERS	NOTABLE OWNERS/OCCUPIERS	CURRENT OWNERSHIP/ OCCUPANCY
No. 31 (north portion)	1st Baron Belasyse	1684–97 Savile family 1728–48 Banks family	
	1748 demolished		
No. 31 (as Norfolk House)	1748–52 (Matthew Brettingham jnr) 1939 rebuilt (Gunton & Gunton) 1976 refurbished (T. P. Bennett & Son)	1748–1938 9th–16th Dukes of Norfolk 1942–44 Allied Force Headquarters 1947–76 British Aluminium Co. (in part Rolls Royce (1975) Ltd)	Freeholders: United Kingdom Provident Institution Tenants: Lamco Paper Sales Ltd Varma Services Ltd Finnboard (UK) Ltd Kymmene Paper Ltd Korn-Ferry International RCA International Ltd A.T. & T. International (UK) Ltd
No. 32	1670 1st Baron Belasyse	1676–88 Anne Countess of Warwick and 10th Earl of Warwick 1710–16 4th Duke of Hamilton and his widow 1729–37 1st Earl of Ashburnham (1732–35 let to Sir Robert Walpole)	Freeholders: Prudential Assurance Co. (since 1949)
	1818 rebuilt C. R. Cockerell	1771–1921 Bishops of London 1921–41 leased, then bought Caledonian Club 1941–82 Under requisition or lease for Govt Departments	Head lessees: Hammerson UK Properties Ltd Sub-tenants: Goddard Kay Rogers & Associates
No. 33	1669–70 1st Baron Belasyse 1752 rebuilt Robert Adam	1678–85 1st Duke of Devonshire 1722–31 6th Earl of Montrath 1734–1806 1st–4th Earls of Buckinghamshire (let 1746–91) 1807–23 1st Earl of St Germans 1841–53 4th Earl of Dartmouth 1854–19 14th–17th Earls of Derby 1910–40 English & Scottish Law Life Assoc. and various commercial tenants (in part Caledonian Club)	
		1942–82 under requisition or lease for Govt Departments (in part National Provincial Bank)	Freeholders: Prudential Assurance Co. (since 1949) Head lessees: Hammerson UK Properties Ltd Sub-tenants: Consolidated Gold Fields

Appendix IIa

The Square, House by House 2001

HOUSE	CHANGES SINCE 1986	CURRENT OCCUPIER
Nos. 1 & 2	Demolished 1994/95. New office building erected on site designed by Sheppard Robson & Partners completed 1998.	Ericsson (Freeholder)
No. 3	-	Veronis Suhler International Limited Apollo Management (UK) LLC Laird Group Kingfisher Management Bancomext Polygram Leisure Limited Breezevale Services Touchstone Securities Ltd Quartz Capital Partners Ltd Matheson (London Properties) Ltd
No. 4	Purchased by Naval & Military Club in 1996 & converted into club premises	Naval & Military Club (Freeholder)
No. 5	-	Kerman & Co Brandeaux Group Tuskar Oil Limited Rio Tinto
No. 6	-	Rio Tinto
No. 7	-	Slater Chapman & Cooke
No. 8	-	Universal Music International
No. 9	-	Royal Institute of International Affairs
No. 10	-	Royal Institute of International Affairs
No. 11	-	Regus Conference Ltd
No. 12	-	Regus Conference Ltd
No. 13	-	U.K.I
No. 14	-	London Library
No. 15	-	Clerical Medical Investment Group Ltd

Appendix IIa - The Square, House by House 2001

HOUSE	CHANGES SINCE 1986	CURRENT OCCUPIER
No. 16	-	East India Club
No. 17	-	East India Club
No. 18	Purchased by Berkeley Homes 1996 and converted into 10 luxury apartments	Private tenants
No. 19	Demolished 1996/97. New office building erected on site designed by Trehearne & Norman Partners Limited	Harewood International (Freeholder) Gleacher & Co Elliott Management The Rolex Watch Company
No. 20	Rear section of building demolished 1989/90 and rebuilt to new design by Hamilton Associates Architects Ltd. Modern replica of Robert Adam courtyard incorporated into the plan. Robert Adam 1770's building tied into new design.	State Street Global Rexiter Capital Managment Ltd J.O. Hambros Investment Management Ltd Miraband Group Justerini & Brooks
No. 21	Rear section of building demolished 1989/90 and rebuilt to new design by Hamilton Associates Architects Ltd. New building tying in with No. 21 grade listed frontage.	Occupation as No. 20
No. 36 Pall Mall	Frontage onto St James's Square	Army & Navy Club
No. 31	Norfolk House	WPM – Kymmene Ltd Weatherall Green & Smith
No. 32	-	Williams Holdings Plc
No. 33	-	HQ Executive Offices (UK) Ltd

Index

ST JAME

Part North and

Part North and E

Part North and E.